PRAISE FOR *PLAN L*

"Dawn's passion and experience for teaching illuminate her brilliantly penned manifesto. She helps you discover your greatness as an educator and guides you through designing extraordinary, purposeful, and life-changing learning journeys that will impact every student far beyond the classroom. You will be captivated by her stories and empowered by her ideas and strategies, which can be applied in any grade level and content area. Get ready to set sail for an incredible adventure with Dawn Harris!"

—Tisha Richmond, student engagement specialist, PD specialist, and author of *Make Learning Magical*

"As you navigate the pages of this gem, you will gain insight from Dawn's expertise with antiracist teaching, explore a planning framework, and discover a plethora of resources to help you meet the needs of every one of your learners. Not only will you glean ideas to create a classroom culture that thrives in all areas of academics, but your mind and heart will be filled with a renewed commitment to making every student feel included and valued. Want to teach with purpose? *Plan Like a PIRATE* is a must-read!"

—Tara Martin, educator and author of *Be REAL: Educate from the Heart* and *Cannonball In*

"This book goes far beyond planning. It charts the reader's destiny to become a great educator. *Plan Like a PIRATE* issues a charge for teachers to grow themselves professionally and become antiracist educators who provide challenging, empathetic, and memorable experiences for our students. Dawn Harris passionately encourages educators to steer their own ships toward the comprehensive personal and professional growth that leads to powerful success and achievement. She shows us that these journeys to greatness have a direct impact on student confidence, achievement, success, and performance. Whether you are a superintendent or a classroom teacher, *Plan Like a PIRATE* is for you. It's for all of us.

I am blessed to have Dawn in my life as a friend, sister, and business partner. Her passion, her commitment to excellence, and her drive for helping others are all woven into the pages of *Plan Like a PIRATE*."

—Traci Browder, MEd, Intelligogy Education Consulting, cofounder of GritCrewEDU

"Great educators make teaching look effortless—but master teachers know that deep learning happens only through intentional design. *Plan Like a PIRATE* shares a roadmap for how to design rich experiences where students engage deeply and critically with content to advance their learning. A master teacher herself, Dawn Harris shares stories from the trenches and weaves in practical strategies and frameworks to help make learning accessible and meaningful for students. This is a must-read for all educators!"

—Jill Siler, EdD, deputy executive director, Texas Association of School Administrators, and author of *Thrive Through the Five: Practical Truths to Powerfully Lead Through Challenging Times*

"Our journey as educational leaders never ends. The goal? To leave a lasting impact on students as we empower them to build their foundations of truth.

In *Plan Like a PIRATE*, Dawn Harris guides us on that journey, showing educators how to transform planning with intention, authenticity, and commitment. Her inspirational insights from personal experience encourage us to keep cultivating antiracist teaching and learning. She attests that this will not be an easy process, yet her charge to readers is that we CAN and WILL do this work with genuine advocacy, passion, and dedication. *Plan Like a PIRATE* is a profound exploration that will leave you anchored with confidence."

—Jillian DuBois, educator and author and illustrator of *Liv's Seashells, Road to Awesome: A Journey for Kids,* and *Look at YOU, Piper Lou!*

"I'm humbled and honored to have been around some great minds in education over the years. Dawn is definitely one of them, and *Plan Like a PIRATE* is her bold manifesto. We sometimes assume that educators intuitively know how to create engaging environments, but that's not always the case. This book looks closely at the specifics of the interactions between educators and learners that create compelling learning experiences. *Plan Like a PIRATE* is more than just a tool for looking at how we structure learning; it teaches us how to create memorable experiences for both the educator and the learner."

—Vernon Wright, speaker, author, consultant, leader

"I absolutely LOVE this extensive, reflective book, which will not only benefit you but your students, their parents, school teams, and the community. This guide not only affirms your PIRATE teaching style, it refines and extends it! It is the compass for navigating your own journey! What are you waiting for? Get your copy, expand your knowledge, reflect on your teaching, and plan your adventure today!"

—Melisa Hayes, second grade teacher

"Dawn Harris is a gifted educator and an amazing human. She gives so much to her profession and students. She is a pioneer in equity work, teaching students how to think, write, and read with purpose. The work and words in *Plan Like a PIRATE* are honest and real. I have been privileged to work with Dawn for many years, and I have learned so much from her generous, authentic spirit, which she's artfully poured into this book."

—April Gunterman, high school intervention specialist

"A truly inspiring must-read for any educator, from preservice to year forty-one! Dawn has masterfully crafted an engaging guide to lead any teacher on the journey to planning rich, meaningful, and inclusive learning experiences for all students. Packed full with practical tips and strategies to enhance professional practice, *Plan Like a PIRATE* is guaranteed to help us all on our personal journeys to greatness in the classroom!"

—Curt Bradshaw, school improvement consultant

"*Plan Like a PIRATE* makes you want to jump in and be the best you can be for the young leaders we see in our schools every day. You will be able to take countless ideas from it to bring students learning that matters to them. In everything from student-led learning and effective differentiation to fostering an antiracist mindset, Dawn Harris provides evidence, tools, and strategies to transform traditional planning into co-created experiences with students. She amplifies the importance of our work in teaching students to be good human beings who hold the power to change our world. *Plan Like a PIRATE* is a book I wish I had when I first started teaching and a resource I'm grateful to have as a veteran teacher."

—Nili Bartley, author of *Lead beyond Your Title*

PLAN LIKE A PIRATE

PLAN LIKE A PIRATE

DESIGNING
Extraordinary Learning Journeys
FOR EVERY STUDENT

DAWN M. HARRIS

Plan Like a PIRATE: Designing Extraordinary Learning Journeys for Every Student
© 2021 Dawn M. Harris

This book is available at special discounts when purchased in quantity for educational purposes or for use as premiums, promotions, or fundraisers. For inquiries and details, contact the publisher at books@daveburgessconsulting.com.

Published by Dave Burgess Consulting, Inc.
San Diego, CA
DaveBurgessConsulting.com

Library of Congress Control Number: 2021944209
Paperback ISBN: 978-1-951600-99-0
Ebook ISBN: 978-1-956306-00-2

Cover and interior design by Liz Schreiter
Edited and produced by Reading List Editorial
ReadingListEditorial.com

*This book is dedicated to my husband, John,
and our son, John Raymond.
I love you both to the moon and back.*

CONTENTS

FOREWORD

By Shelley Burgess

One of the most frustrating experiences I had as an educational leader occurred when I was a relatively new principal. I worked in a community where the majority of students we welcomed into our schools were English language learners. As a result, English language development (ELD) was understandably an essential component of our curriculum. The district-wide plan and the classroom curriculum being used to support our learners as they developed English skills were not proving to be very effective.

So a committee was put together to create a new plan. This was important work, and there was a lot of good learning that came out of it. However, one outcome was that our district ultimately decided to purchase a scripted curriculum to be used to teach ELD to our students.

The curriculum was piloted at one of our schools, and I remember the principal of that school sharing how much she loved the new program. She told us that it was so well scripted that she had been able to create extremely small ELD groups because anyone could teach it as long as they followed the script. So, just about anyone did "teach" ELD: teachers, of course, but also aides, volunteers, custodians, and who knows who else. She sang the praises of this program.

The more she shared, the more frustrated and, honestly, the more heartbroken I became.

How was it possible that we had arrived at a place where we thought the best way to teach our students such an essential set of skills was to hand someone—anyone—a script and tell them to follow it exactly for thirty to forty-five minutes a day? Was that really what someone believed good teaching was? A committee of people telling teachers not to "teach" but just to read and follow the instructions in a script?

Teaching is incredibly complex. Do great teachers need to have an in-depth understanding of their content? Of course they do, but that is merely a starting point. Beyond depth of content knowledge, teaching also requires the precise use of effective instructional practices, the wise allocation of resources, and an understanding of assessments and how to use them along with long-term planning and short-term adjustments. It involves knowing the unique learning needs of each student and developing strategies to reach them and help them thrive. Exceptional teaching is a commitment to equity and social justice. It involves grit, determination, persistence, flexibility, an element of fun, and a whole lot of heart. No program has that kind of magic, but great teachers do.

Dawn Harris knows this, and in *Plan Like a PIRATE*, she proves that great teaching doesn't happen by accident, and it can't be found in a script. Great teaching—PIRATE teaching—happens on purpose because we *plan* for it. It is a choice we make to be meticulous, intentional, and thorough as we guide our students to fulfill their greatest potential as both learners and human beings who contribute to our world as a whole.

To know Dawn is to know her passion for her students and for both the art and science of teaching. But beyond that, she has a passion and drive to constantly improve, to set goals and to crush them. She is the kind of teacher whose very last day of teaching before she leaves the classroom will be her best ever, because she continues to commit to being better tomorrow than today. As a reader of *Plan Like a PIRATE*, you are the beneficiary of the many years she's dedicated to becoming an exceptional educator. She has poured her heart, soul, experience, and expertise into this book. From her CHART a course to a better world philosophy, her dedication to antiracist teaching, her redefining of our roles as "Chief Engagement Officers," her framework of Eight Essential Practices to plan for every day, and so much more, there is something for every educator in this book.

As you scour the pages of *Plan Like a PIRATE,* Dawn will guide your steps to your own greatness as an educator. She will introduce you to ideas that will help you prepare students for rich academic lives *and* rich lives beyond the classroom walls full of compassion and joy. And she will help make sure you do it on purpose!

INTRODUCTION

The world *becomes a better place because of your greatness.*
—DAVE BURGESS

When I was a little girl, I used to love playing school. Even back then, I was a planner at heart. I remember lining up my stuffed animals and dolls all around my bedroom, which I had magically transformed into a fully functioning classroom. I had a small easel-style chalkboard for teaching spelling and math, and I would beg my mother and my grandmother to bring me papers from every place they went—any kind of form, document, booklet—anything that I could use as pretend activities for my wide-eyed, well-behaved "students" (the "naughty kids" had to sit in the corner). When Mom and Grandma didn't deliver, I would draw my own worksheets, filling them up with empty squares and fill-in-the-blank lines that my imaginary class would complete with their imaginary answers. I put *X*s on incorrect "answers" and stars on the best of those blank but detailed "graphic organizers."

Even at six or seven years old, I tried as best I could to replicate my own school experience in my imaginary classroom through meticulous planning, but I didn't really know then that I was a *planner*. All I knew was that I wanted to be a great teacher, and I wanted my students to be good students who could show me all that they had learned. I've come a long way since my childhood teaching gig, thank goodness. I've learned so much about what it means to be a great teacher.

But, long after I left my childhood "job," I remained a planner. For me, designing actionable steps to bring a thing to fruition has always been a challenge of sorts—almost an obsession! Tell me you need something to happen, and I'll create a dynamic plan to deliver the goods. I still plan everything I can get my hands into: parties, trips, lessons, training and development for others, and my own personal and professional growth. When my son was little, I would begin organizing elaborate birthday parties for him months early, complete with the coolest cakes, exciting games, and awesome entertainment, resulting in the most wonderful party a kid could imagine. I'm sure my friends and family (maybe even my son!) thought I was a little outrageous with my planning, but I wanted everyone in attendance, especially my boy, to have a memorable time. I wanted his parties to be extraordinary.

I feel the same way about planning learning for my students. I want their experiences in my classroom to last a lifetime. I want their learning to be momentous, something they will carry with them long after they leave my classroom. Every day when students enter that room, I want them to know I have taken the time to design a journey for them that will be like no other. From the moment I entered my very first classroom many years ago, my goal was to be the best teacher and the best planner I could possibly be.

THE JOURNEY FROM "SEEING IT" TO "BEING IT"

There are many qualities we can attach to great teaching. Great teachers make students feel like they can do or be anything. They make their students feel loved no matter who they are. They make students feel as if they belong. They show students how to be resilient, how to overcome adversity, and how to fall in love with learning. They give students a voice they never knew they had. They set high expectations but provide the support students need to help meet them. Great teachers hold their students and themselves accountable. They teach with a voracious desire to help students grow as learners because they know the education they provide their students has the ability to transform their students' lives and may even help them escape what might be painful or dangerous circumstances. Great teachers invest much of their time and energy into finding ways to foster a love of learning in their students, offering them insights into the power of hope through the very lessons they teach. And, probably most important of all, great teachers help their students find purpose, to discover ways of attaining the lives they dream of having some day. Great teachers help break cycles, and they help students find new beginnings every day of the year.

GREAT TEACHERS INVEST MUCH OF THEIR TIME AND ENERGY INTO FINDING WAYS TO FOSTER A LOVE OF LEARNING.

Throughout this book, we'll dive deep into the many facets of great teaching through the exploration of the strategies, practices, attitudes, and skills that ensure we're striving for greatness every day we set foot in our classrooms. As you explore the pages of this book, you'll be encouraged to engage in your own reflections about great teaching, and in doing so, you'll gain insights and understandings about what great teaching looks like as you work toward setting your own personal goals. This is important, because in order to be great, you must have a clear vision of the kind of great you wish to be.

DESTINATION: GREATNESS

Before becoming a professionally licensed educator, I spent quite a few years working in a job I didn't love at all. I grinded away my days in the private sector as a marketing manager, and while that job helped me pay the bills, I went to work every day with a sense of dread. I finally decided that job was not for me. I wanted to find a career where I would have the opportunity to feel like I was making a difference for someone or something. Becoming a teacher would be my chance at that, and I wasn't going to waste it. When I was finally able to enter the classroom, I was determined that I was going to love coming into school every day, and since then, I have. You see, I was intentional about creating the kind of career I wanted this time, and that intentionality and planning has led me to many successes in this career. From blogging about teaching and learning in the context of my own practice, I moved to publishing articles in educational journals and magazines. Alongside my career in secondary education, I became an associate professor of teacher education in Dayton, Ohio, where I used my classroom experience to support preservice teachers as they prepared to enter classrooms themselves. I also took advantage of every opportunity to present training and development workshops at local to international conferences, and from this, I was able to form my own consulting firm to support schools and organizations as they strive to meet the needs of their students. I've done all of this while teaching because teaching is the fuel behind everything I do. This fuel—my passion for teaching—also helps energize my students. When we are together, we are on fire. I tell you this because all of this is possible for you, too. I want every teacher to not just reach but to exceed their goals, because when we strive for greatness, our students will strive for greatness, too.

PROFESSIONAL GROWTH IS PART OF THE PLAN

In defining the vision of greatness we seek to achieve, we should also never settle into the mindset that we are as good as we are ever going to get—at anything. In fact, it is my belief that, as teachers, this kind of thinking can be detrimental to our success. The real truth is that greatness is a moving target, and we should always be aiming for it. In education, the landscape changes daily, sometimes by the minute. Our kids, our classes, schools, policies, curriculum, all shift so rapidly that it often seems we are in a constant state of flux. With this constant metamorphosis that *is* education, we should find that we continually need to transform ourselves to account for this routine change. We should also understand that it's simply not okay to accept mediocrity—it's not okay for us, it's not okay for our schools, and it's certainly not okay for our students. Being mediocre doesn't challenge us and it definitely doesn't change us, and this won't suffice when the world around us is rapidly evolving itself. Every teacher must therefore have a clear and malleable plan for how to move beyond average and work toward greatness. We owe it to our students, and we owe it to ourselves.

The bottom line is this: those who focus on their own professional growth excel. Dave Burgess, author of *Teach Like a PIRATE*, says it best: "The *world* becomes a better place because of your greatness." Truer words have never been spoken, and those words apply utterly to the concept behind this book. With just the right plan and a solid commitment to accomplishing our professional goals, we can become teachers who don't just change students, but teachers who change the world.

BECOMING A PIRATE PLANNER

You might have figured out by now that this book is not simply about lesson planning (although there is a bit of that in here!). Instead, this is a book about growth and performance—yours as well as that of your students. Think of this as a guidebook of sorts that will take you through the process of planning your own journey to teaching greatness so that your students and others around you are inspired to aim for greatness, too. If you're a PIRATE teacher already, then you know that your **passion** as an educator, **immersing** students in content, building **rapport** with your students, **asking** yourself and your students questions, **analyzing** information, focusing on **transformation**, and remaining **enthusiastic** in all things are critical elements of student engagement and empowerment. PIRATE planning supplements these practices by helping us to create designs for learning that allow us to actively and continuously develop and refine our methods for reaching kids in ways that result in great teaching, plain and simple. So, if you don't yet know what it is to be a PIRATE teacher, then your very next task is to *run* to the closest bookstore or log on to Amazon and grab yourself a copy of Dave Burgess's renowned book *Teach Like a PIRATE*. Not only will you gain a clear vision of what engaging and creative teaching looks like, but you will also be empowered to jump right into designing the kind of great teaching that *Plan Like a PIRATE* guides you toward, the kind of teaching your students need *and* deserve!

PIRATE planners relentlessly explore every possible avenue to reach kids. They show up every day with a strategy for helping students arrive at their own desired destinations in life. PIRATE planners ensure not only that each day brings a new adventure in learning for students, but that students come thirsty for that adventure. Students of PIRATE planners know that their teachers are focused on delivering engaging, relevant learning experiences that they will use every day of their lives, no matter the content or subject matter. PIRATE planners know that the horizon of learning shifts regularly and that if they have any hope of successfully navigating the sometimes turbulent waters of their classroom, they must chart a course that keeps everyone sailing toward their own unique destination even amid the choppiest of waters.

I guess you could say this book serves as my own manifesto of sorts, as it includes the methods, strategies, and approaches I have taken that have helped me to become an accomplished educator over the years. For example, as a PIRATE planner, I invite students to focus on their attitudes, values, and beliefs in the context of learning in our classroom. I invite students to participate in learning that is inclusive, student centered, and antiracist. The PIRATE planning framework of nonnegotiable practices that this book provides has helped me over the years to craft the most engaging lessons students could hope for—the kind that fosters in them a love of learning because of the carefully differentiated experiences I strive to create for them. My hope is that this book reveals to you a road map for the teaching career you've always dreamed of, one that will ignite, or reignite, your passion for teaching as you explore the processes of deepening your practice and powering up your professionalism both inside and outside of school. If you are looking for a plan to help guide you to greatness in the classroom, you are in the right place.

The Commitment to Antiracist Teaching and Learning

I have always been an educator focused on bringing social justice, empathy, and tolerance to the forefront of learning in my content area, but in 2018, I had to make a drastic shift in my focus to meet an immediate need. That year, I took deliberate steps to bring a group of junior high students on a journey of discovery through an extended unit of study centering on racism and American civil rights history. My reason for doing so was triggered by the fact that I had begun to see a shift in the ways in which certain Americans were being openly treated, Americans who did not fit into the box that contained the dominant culture in this country. The rhetoric toward immigrants, Muslims, Black victims of police brutality, and even social activists had turned dangerously sour, and those attitudes were beginning to spill over into my classroom. It broke my heart to hear the repetition of hateful dialogue some students had picked up from home or on social media play out in the conversations in my classroom.

Early in that school year, I took a detour from my original plans and made a shift in my classroom teaching that I now know has had lasting impact on both me and my students. I decided to break the rules and put aside my curriculum map to put forth a new plan that took students on an exploration of the voices, experiences, events, and perspectives from pre–Civil War America to the current year. For several months, in the context of English language arts, my eighth-grade students explored the events that led to the Civil War. We read and talked about Lincoln and the Gettysburg Address and about Frederick Douglass. We debated and discussed our way through Reconstruction and Jim Crow, to the modern civil rights movement. Students learned about the Montgomery Bus Boycott, Emmett Till, the Little Rock Nine, the Greensboro sit-ins, the Birmingham Children's Crusade, the Voting Rights Act, and more. We studied all the way from October to March, and for a culminating activity, my students created projects that they shared at our local university with preservice educators about to enter the field. Some students even had the chance to visit the National Underground Railroad Freedom Center in Cincinnati, Ohio, where they were able to learn more about the stories and people we had explored together in class.

It was a great unit. I was proud of all that my students had learned; however, it wasn't an easy task at the time, and it certainly is not the way I approach teaching as an antiracist educator now. You see, it wasn't that I hadn't considered up to that point the fact that students needed to be aware of their own biases, or that I had to show students the effects of both individualized and systemic racism; it was just that I found myself staring at a sea of mostly white faces thinking, *I'm Black. How in the world am I going to pull this off?* I wasn't sure how my white students would respond to my actions, but I had no choice. I had to take the leap and commit to transforming my curriculum to help students understand the effects racism has on all of us. What I did back then was a response to what I felt was a moment of crisis, but what I came to realize was that I would need to change the way I taught if I was going to help my students out of the kind of thinking that kept them unaware of the impacts of individual and systemic racism and their roles in it. From that point forward, my goal was to make sure that at any given moment in my practice I would find ways to bring students to a greater understanding about racism, injustice, inequity, and the value of their own actions in working to dismantle these things.

I have to admit, my journey to becoming an actively antiracist educator only truly began as a result of this experience with my students. Since then, I have made antiracist teaching and learning a permanent focus of my growth and development because the more I work toward this goal, the more I realize there is to understand about the impacts of all types of racism on our kids and on our schools. Through antiracist teaching, I continue to learn things about myself, my students, and society that bring me to new understandings each and every day. Looking at the world through an actively antiracist lens will do that for you. Becoming an antiracist educator has been life changing for me. I made the commitment to making it life changing for my students, too.

I have learned much about myself and what I am capable of as an antiracist educator, especially as a Black biracial educator. I know the anxiousness that comes with courageously tackling tough issues with kids because they needed me to guide them through those issues, but I also know the joy that comes from seeing students beautifully navigate challenging conversations. I know what it feels like to be alone in the task of creating an antiracist curriculum and classroom, but I've also experienced being surrounded by a professional learning community (PLC) filled with allies united together with the goal of transforming schools into antiracist ones. I've learned that while we can be allies and advocates for those silenced, we cannot force others to do the same. Becoming an antiracist educator is a personal decision that one must be willing to come to on their own and with their own reasons for doing so. All I can say is that there is no more room for excuses from any of us as to why we are not taking proactive steps to create safe, inclusive, antiracist learning environments for every student in every school.

Antiracist teaching and learning is not for the faint of heart, but we are teachers and faint of heart is one thing we are not. And if a lone Black teacher can do this with classrooms full of white students, then white teachers can do the same. This is the only time you will ever hear me tell my white colleagues to use your privilege, but, friends, you have to. If you are in a position to use your privilege to reach students, then do it. Be relentless in telling students the truths about racism they need to hear. It may not sound any different coming from you than from me, but it may *feel* different. And that matters. You may encounter resistant students, parents, and even peers who don't support what you are doing. You may even think, *Goodness, I hope I'm doing this right*, doubting whether you've come far enough in your own antiracist education to be qualified to guide others in theirs; but with time, effort, and focus, you can be great at this just like you are great at everything else you do in your classroom.

What I share with you in this book is far from the complete process of becoming an actively antiracist educator, not by a long shot, but the strategies provided here will get you started. You will plan, you will experiment, you'll try, and you will fail, but I promise you will grow into an educator who knows that our world can't afford to accept the kinds of attitudes and behaviors that foster hate and division and that sow inequity. We know better, so we need to do better. As James Baldwin said, we "must be prepared to 'go for broke'"[1] when educating children on the ugly realities of racism.

The commitment to antiracism education and equity is a lifelong one. It is not something you will fulfill in a semester or even a school year. With this in mind, you can confidently begin tailoring a plan that will help transform your classroom into a safe, equitable, and aware learning space that values the cultures, the voices, and the beliefs of all people no matter who they are.

---

1   James Baldwin, "A Talk to Teachers," speech, October 16, 1963, reprinted on richgibson
     .com/talktoteachers.htm.

PLANNING YOUR JOURNEY TO GREATNESS

Within this book, the pathway to great teaching has been clearly outlined for you, all the way from how to build a solid foundation for learning to creating antiracist classrooms to discovering how to use all of your knowledge, expertise, and passion to design an outstanding career for yourself. Once you have read through the sections, you will have an arsenal of practical yet powerful strategies that will help you move from simply envisioning greatness to being able to share your greatness with the world. Here is a glimpse of what you will find inside these pages:

Part I. See It: The Design behind Great Teaching

In part one of this book, you will explore the idea that who we are as teachers can have a tremendous impact on our students. You'll be challenged to think about the kind of teacher you wish to be for kids so that you can develop a plan to work toward that vision every day. And, when you CHART a course to a better world through the integration of curiosity, hope, advocacy, responsibility, and trust into all you teach, you'll be helping to prepare students for successful lives beyond your classroom. In these chapters, you will see a design for great teaching emerge so that you can begin planning your own journey to greatness. Here, we will launch the discussion of what it looks like when we commit to creating antiracist classrooms for kids.

Part II. Plan It: Deepen Your Practice

Part two introduces you to your new title of CEO, chief engagement officer of your classroom, and you'll receive helpful strategies for building a platform for engagement that will set kids on fire for learning. You'll be introduced to methods for overcoming obstacles as you work to become an antiracist educator, and you will learn to backward-design differentiated learning targets that will guarantee you are reaching every student.

Part III. Do It: Implement with Precision

In part three of this book, you'll dive into an exploration of the Essential Eight, a framework for teaching that will transform the learning you design into memorable and exciting experiences for students as you help them navigate their own learning journeys. You'll gain new insights into what it takes to become an educator who fully embeds antiracist teaching and learning into your everyday practice, and you will also get to see a sample project unit that embodies all of the characteristics of PIRATE planning. By the end of this section, you will have a clear plan for strengthening your practice and catapulting yourself and your students into greatness!

Part IV. Be It: Own Your Success

In the last section of *Plan Like a PIRATE*, you'll dig deep into the actions necessary to push yourself forward professionally. This section will help you learn to embrace the evaluation process and to see it as your opportunity to shine a spotlight on the great teacher you have become. You'll also examine how professional learning communities and networks can help you find your purpose as an educator and how important it is to share your brilliance with the world by pushing yourself toward becoming a leader in your field, even if you don't have a formal title as one. In this final portion of the book, you'll be encouraged to possess a mindset that is ever focused on infinitely reimagining education, for yourself and for your students.

DROP ANCHOR

On any great trip, there are destinations along the way where we get to stop and spend time enjoying the beauty of our journey. Through chapter six of this book, at the end of each chapter, this is exactly what the Drop Anchor sections are designed to do: allow time for you to pause and reflect on where you've been and assess how far you have to go to reach your greatness goals. In these sections, you will explore insightful questions that invite you to think critically about each chapter's contents in order to plan your journey to becoming a great teacher. Consider these moments snapshots of your experiences and understandings that you can refer back to or that you can revisit in order to reflect again whenever you need to.

SAIL ON

In the Sail On sections at the ends of chapters seven and eight, you will take time to contemplate where your teaching journey takes you next. As you will have spent time in the preceding chapters reframing your teaching mindset and revisiting how you plan your practice, the Sail On sections give you the chance to think ahead to fully realizing greatness in your teaching career. Whether it's employing the strategies in this book to improve your performance evaluations or taking action to share your expertise with the world, these opportunities to Sail On will challenge you and help steer you toward bigger and better destinations in the classroom and beyond.

PLAN LIKE A PIRATE ON THE WEB

Please take time throughout your journey to visit my website, www.educationundone.com. There, you will find an abundance of materials to support you as you grow into a PIRATE planner. Just click the "Plan Like a PIRATE" tab and you'll have immediate access to many of the tools and resources mentioned in this book, including:

- Downloadable PIRATE planning templates
- Printable posters and downloadable digital media
- Printable journal pages
- Course offerings
- Antiracism education resource library

- The *Plan Like a PIRATE* book study guide
- Workshop and booking information
- PIRATE planner merch, and more!

In addition to visiting my website, feel free to use the #PlanLAP hashtag on your favorite social media platforms, including Twitter, Instagram, and Facebook. Take time to encourage others by sharing your insights, growth, and reflections with the world as you journey toward greatness in PIRATE style!

ARE YOU READY?

The journey to greatness is a commitment. You must be willing to put in the time and energy necessary to move toward being the best teacher possible for your students and for yourself. Perhaps you wish to

- Heighten the sense of community and belonging in your classroom
- Design better lessons and more engaging activities
- Create environments that have students on fire for learning
- Become an accomplished educator, securing the best evaluations every time
- Build strong relationships with students and your peers in education
- Redesign your planning to include antiracist teaching and learning
- Expand your practice to help other educators grow from your experiences

If you *are* ready, begin chronicling your journey by writing your commitment statement here or by using the resources you'll find on the *Plan Like a PIRATE* webpage in the Introduction section. As you craft your statement, incorporate powerful verbs such as *inspire, create, discover, design, thrive,* and *transform.* Think about the impact you wish to have on students, who you are as a person and as a teacher, and what you wish to become, as well as the purpose you seek to live out each day.

I'm ready to begin my journey to greatness because . . .

_____

_____

_____

_____

_____

I will commit to growing on this journey by . . .

_____

_____

_____

_____

_____

In doing so, I hope to . . .

_____

_____

_____

_____

_____

DROP ANCHOR

- What does it mean for you, for your students, and for your profession if you relentlessly strive to be great in your classroom and even beyond?

- Imagine a vision of the classroom you wish to have, of the teacher you wish to be, of the joy and success you wish for your students to experience each day. Write down your vision. Pin it up somewhere you will see it often. Be ready and willing to do whatever it takes to make that vision reality.

- How do your current views about race and racism help or hinder your growth toward becoming an antiracist educator? What implicit biases do you have that you will need to identify and come to terms with so that you are able to become a champion of antiracism? What is your strategy for overcoming your own biases or lack of awareness?

- Take one small action every day that will move you toward that vision of greatness. Keep track of your journey by recording your reflections in a journal or by blogging about your growth and development and sharing it with others.

PART I

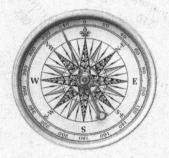

See It

THE DESIGN BEHIND GREAT TEACHING

ONE

Prepare To Make an Impact

> *There are two kinds of teachers: the kind that fill you with so much quail shot that you can't move, and the kind that just gives you a little prod behind and you jump to the skies.*
> —ROBERT FROST

Many years ago, I found myself barely surviving what were some terrible high school years. I had moved between three different high schools over the course of four years, all in opposite corners of Ohio, due to my stepfather's line of work. I was uprooted amid some very painful mental health issues that my parents most likely didn't even know about. I suffered extreme insomnia due to anxiety issues for more than three of those four years. When I got to school, all I did was sleep. My mother navigated my situation the best she could, but no one really told her the extent of what was going on—not me, and definitely not any of my teachers. To say that my high school life was a mess would have been an extreme understatement.

When I arrived at the last high school I would attend as a student—in a school district whose mascot, ironically, was a pirate!—I quickly discovered the impact that a great teacher could have on her students. Before, in a different school district, I learned how easy it can be to slip through the cracks in classrooms where great teaching is *not* a priority.

A TALE OF TWO TEACHERS

Julie

It was in eleventh grade that I met Julie, my very first PIRATE teacher, literally and figuratively. She was someone who helped change the trajectory of my life at that time. She taught me how to feel passionate about school again and how to find joy in coming there every day. I looked forward to her energy, to catching it, so I could let go of the pain even if it was for just a little bit while I was in her care.

Julie was my art teacher, and I remember her face as clear as the screen I'm looking at while I type these words. I can see her twinkling eyes, her smile that lit up the room. She was always happy to see *all of us*, every single student in her class. She greeted us with hugs or high fives. She was a bright spot in our day, and as an eleventh grader, I thought she was totally cool for a grown-up. She always bounced around the room like Tinkerbell, spreading joy everywhere.

In class, Julie circulated around every table in our art room looking at every creation, offering feedback laced with compliments and encouragement. In the midst of doing so, she held personal conversations and genuinely strived to build relationships with her students. She connected on an entirely different level than other teachers. She encouraged us to enter contests and think about art as a career or how to connect what we were doing in her class to what was happening in our other classes like social studies or math. Yes, in math! I hated math until I learned how important it is to art. She gave us a new lens through which to look at other learning.

Mr. Black

Mr. Black was my English teacher. Throughout all my years in school, I loved reading, and in those challenging high school years, I especially craved the escape from my anxiety that reading brought me. Sadly, though, I never felt Mr. Black's passion for reading and literature in the way that Julie set my heart on fire for learning about art. Because of this, I felt no connection, no desire to learn about my favorite subject when I was in Mr. Black's classroom.

In Mr. Black's class there was just sitting, lots and lots of sitting. We all sat, Mr. Black included. The room was traditionally arranged in columns and rows, and there was little to no collaboration between students. Feedback arrived in red or green ink. The color I saw most was red: on my paper, and on my face—sometimes from anger, but mostly from embarrassment. Mr. Black's red ink made me feel like a failure. I remember the dread associated with entering his room and my quick drift into slumber that always followed shortly after I got there.

I was far from Mr. Black's favorite student. I know this. I don't think he ever said my name outside of taking attendance at the start of class. But Mr. Black also never asked me to wake up. No gentle nudge. No shout from the front of the class. No book slammed on my desk. He never asked me why I was sleeping or if anything was wrong. He never asked me why I struggled to get my work done or, when I did, why it was so terrible. He just routinely delivered that bright red ink. All error, no feedback.

To this day, I don't know for sure if Mr. Black had a plan for his students each day. If he did, I don't know what they looked like, but I do know they didn't include me. I'm sure that was true for other students in his class, yet there were probably students who enjoyed Mr. Black's class, too. As a teacher myself, I now know that we not only *can* plan our practice to include all students (even the challenging ones), but we *must* plan that way. The consequences of not doing so means we will lose some students, and neither we nor our students can afford for that to happen.

Julie Was a PIRATE Teacher

What I didn't know then that I know now is that Julie was a true PIRATE teacher. She embodied all of the elements that lead to engaging and exciting classroom experiences that stick with students for a lifetime. Julie committed herself to her work because she knew kids were counting on her and she wasn't going to let them down, no matter what.

In true PIRATE fashion, Julie demonstrated **passion** in her work every day, and that enthusiasm for her profession and her content radiated from everything she said and did. She was an artist, and her goal was to show us our own potential for becoming artists, too.

Julie **immersed** us in content, and in doing so, she was able to weave her own passion into every single thing she taught us. Never once did we know anything other than this was art class and we were there to be great at it. She made it her job to take us down any and all avenues that would help us do just that.

Julie had a fantastic **rapport** with every one of her students. I never saw her angry or upset with students, because she never had to be. Her classroom management was on point. She showed us respect, and we showed respect in return. She believed in accountability and second chances, and most importantly, she believed in us.

Although I never personally saw her do it, I know without a doubt that Julie regularly engaged in ideation while planning learning for her class. She must have **asked** herself questions about the many ways she could reach every student in art class, and she most certainly had to **analyze** the outcomes of the learning that occurred in her class. It would be easy to assume that because Julie was an art teacher, she was, by default, creative in her lesson planning. What I can say confidently is that whatever she did during her planning helped us to be better artists and better people. She challenged us in so many ways pertaining to our creativity, and that took work. She questioned us relentlessly: Why did you choose that color? Why did you place that object there? What might happen if you moved this object or put a curve here, a shadow there? She showed us the possibilities that lay before us in our work. She helped us to see that with every action there was a consequence, not just in our artwork, but in life, too. She was a master at helping us to be better thinkers, which made us better at, well, everything.

Through her planning and teaching, Julie **transformed** our thinking about art, about school, about our own value as individuals, and about what we could do with our lives: exactly whatever we wanted. She was far more than an art teacher. Julie was a source of inspiration for so many of us. That inspiration led us to believe that our dreams were never out of reach.

Enthusiasm emanated from every single thing Julie did, before, during, and even at the end of class. She was enthusiastic in the hallways and when I stopped in after school to say goodbye for the day. Enthusiasm seeped from every part of her. This mattered. Her excitement brought me and others excitement, and for those fifty minutes of the day, that was a game changer. No matter how I felt when I was in another classroom, I knew when I got to art class, things would be okay.

For me, Julie went down in the history books as the best teacher I ever had, and I bet if you ask any other student who had Julie in high school all those years ago, many of them would say the same thing. Simply put, Julie was a great teacher. Teaching like this doesn't happen by accident. It happens on purpose because **PIRATE teachers plan for that kind of greatness**. Julie *planned* for every single day she walked into our classroom. She chose her actions carefully. She was meticulous and intentional. She knew that every step she took would have some impact on us, the students she taught. That's a heavy load to carry, but the best teachers bear it every day.

UNMISTAKABLE IMPACT

I tell my story not to belittle or judge the Mr. Blacks of the world, not really even to celebrate the amazing teacher Julie was—well, maybe a little! It is to tell you a true story about the existence of two profoundly different teachers who had an equally profound impact on one student. One was transformative, and the other was excruciating.

Students enter classrooms filled with Julies and Mr. Blacks every day, and the effects each teacher has on them is far reaching. How we choose to plan for and interact with our students has the potential for both good and bad consequences. When we take time to ensure that students are at the center of our instruction, that we have made the effort to get to know them, and that we have planned learning that meets their needs, the chances our impact will be transformative drastically improves.

Becoming a great teacher includes setting goals for yourself, yes, but even before that it begins with the goals you have for your students. In *Teach Like a PIRATE*, Dave Burgess asserts that putting in extra time and effort really won't earn you much more money but that, for educators, "striving for greatness is the ultimate act of unselfishness." This means when our students come to us, we must be ready to deliver on our promises of helping them fulfill their dreams. We'd better bring all we've got when working to meet the learning needs of our students, so as to put their goals above all else. It doesn't matter what others think about our desire to be great. What matters is our own attitude toward becoming the best teacher we can be for our students.

WHAT MATTERS IS OUR OWN ATTITUDE TOWARD BECOMING THE BEST TEACHER WE CAN BE FOR OUR STUDENTS.

Great teaching begins with you—the passion *you* have for your students, your love of the content *you* teach, and even the legacy *you* wish to leave behind. No doubt, you will leave a mark on students' lives. You just need to ask yourself if that mark will be a scar or something that leaves students with memories of inspiration, empowerment, encouragement, and love?

DROP ANCHOR

Reflect on your own "Tale of Two Teachers" and the impact each had on you as a student. Use the chart below to recall your experience with the best and worst teachers you've encountered throughout your education. Did you have a Julie? Who was your Mr. Black? Did they leave you with scars or something else?

Your Julie	Your Mr. Black

Their Impact on You	

✕ Do all of your students know that you have their best interest at heart? How do you know? How will you plan to ensure all students know you care about them as individuals and that they are not just names in your gradebook?

✕ Define some steps to becoming an impactful educator. What actions will you take to make sure students leave your classroom feeling loved, inspired, and encouraged rather than hopeless, helpless, or scarred?

TWO

CHART a Course to a Better World

> *How wonderful it is that nobody need*
> *wait a single moment before starting*
> *to improve the world.*
>
> —ANNE FRANK

When we first decided to become teachers, we chose our desired content area and grade level most likely because of our passion for it. Perhaps that choice came from the fact that we loved and had excelled in a particular subject area when we were in school, or we remembered how much we loved our teacher from our favorite year of school. Many of us chose the teaching profession for reasons that go beyond our enthusiasm for our content or grade band. We chose to become teachers because we love kids. We love seeing them blossom and grow in our classrooms. We love seeing their smiling faces and knowing our students feel safe in our care. We love the fact that they love us as much as we love them.

I think we can all agree that great teaching embodies far more than just placing content in front of our students. Great teaching is also showing our students how to put that content in the context of their own lives so that it will help them grow into better people and into productive, responsible citizens. To help students develop into the kinds of individuals who are capable of making the world a better place, we have to figure out how we can push content-area learning beyond just knowledge and skill building and toward life application.

If we want students to be able to reach their full potential, there are certain elements we must integrate into all of the teaching we do. With that same intentionality we had when we chose our path in education, we absolutely must connect curiosity, hope, advocacy, responsibility, and tolerance (CHART) to the learning experiences we design for our students. These five elements will help transform students' thinking about the world around them and will show students there is another side of learning that stretches beyond the daily content with which we invite them to interact. Together, these elements serve as the DNA of great teaching.

When we design learning through a lens that involves teaching beyond our content, it means we are serious about preparing students for a life beyond the classroom. We have to be committed to taking steps to ensure that our content provides students access to the skill sets that also allow them to live compassionate, joy-filled lives. We owe it to them to teach them how to contribute to a society in which there are endless possibilities and space for everyone to exist peacefully together. When we take time in our lessons to CHART a course to a better world, we are guiding students toward becoming change agents who will shape an unimaginably beautiful future for all of us.

CURIOSITY

Regardless of what you call it—a feeling, a skill, a superpower—curiosity is the key to the kind of thinking that can transform a classroom, a generation, a society, even the world. Curiosity is often the force behind change, and it can help with the discovery of solutions to problems new and old.

Curious students without a doubt become more knowledgeable and, thus, more successful when it comes to learning, both in school and out of it. A sense of curiosity aids in the development of empathy and fosters an openness to understanding others. Armed with the desire for information, curious students are able to push through uncertainty because they are driven to dive deep for the answers they need that will bring them clarity. Finding ways to instill a sense of curiosity in our students should be part of every teacher's plan. We must nurture students to become curious thinkers and learners, as they will grow more drastically because we did.

The Quest for Better Solutions

Curiosity is an individual experience. It should always be our goal to guide students in how to search for answers and find solutions to the issues that matter to *them*. Students may share interests with one another, but their own interests are what will lead them to the information for which they thirst. Curiosity is the avenue through which we engage students in the kind of critical thinking that guarantees they will grow intellectually.

While it is important that we provide students the opportunity to demonstrate mastery of content-related skills in our classrooms, in that same way, we must also allow students the space to explore the ideas that mystify them. Allowing students to form their own questions in the context of our content is not only a true example of student-centered learning, but it also stokes the flames of curiosity— curiosity that is vital to engagement, engagement that leads to action, and action that drives change. Curious students understand that they have the ability to uncover the answers that just might fix all that is wrong with their world.

CHART the Way to Curiosity

Teach students to use the Three Ws. I enjoy having the "I'm sorry" conversation with my students each year, in which I explain to students how sorry I am that somewhere along the line adults implored them to stop asking why. The funny thing is, when I talk with students about this, they know exactly what I'm referring to. They express frustration about how since they were little they have often been turned away when all they seek are answers. I tell them that in our classroom, we are going to reincarnate the question *why*. I tell them I want them to question everything they are curious about. Students are allowed to ask the Three Ws at any time: *What if, I wonder*, and *Why*. If the questions are in context, we are usually able to explore them in real time. Students help one another find the answers they need through discussion, research, background knowledge, and, sometimes, good old logic. This generally doesn't take long, but when it does, we often find that we have all learned a tremendous amount from the exploration that takes place. I do understand that covering our content is important, but if students don't have reason to care about that content, then getting to it won't matter anyway. Allowing students time to be curious can spur the engagement and interest needed to build the skills you're going after in the first place.

Allow students time to daydream, literally. So, what about those other questions students have that aren't related to the content? That's what goes on the Daydream List. Have students keep a list either in paper journals or in Google Docs where they can record the things they are curious about that aren't directly tied to the content. Make time periodically to allow students to mentally engage with the questions they have written there. You might facilitate this practice weekly or biweekly, but either way, if you are going to encourage students to become more curious, you've got to give them time to act on their curiosities. A daydreaming session might involve some smooth music, low lights, and journals, Chromebooks, or other technology where students can record their thoughts. Students can think and research as much or as little as they like. These sessions can last about ten to fifteen minutes and require students to complete a quick written debrief at the end. Together, the class has the opportunity to discuss their questions and any answers they found, or they can ask others for input. You will find that students thoroughly enjoy this process, even though it is challenging at first for them to train their minds to avoid distraction. Guidelines are important: no sleeping, no distracting others, and they have to remain on task if they are using technology.

Intrigue students with interesting stories and facts. Make it a goal, regardless of your content area, to bring students intriguing information from a variety of sources. Include headlines about weird science findings. Invite them to read articles that include odd statistics and data and discuss the impact of that information. For example, did you know that, according to a survey conducted by Sleepopolis and One Poll, more than one-third of adults still sleep with a comfort object?[1] Students may at first be shocked by this interesting fact, but their minds might then shift to thoughts like *Why* or *Wow, I guess I'm not so weird after all.* This kind of information can also lead students to think of ideas that offer solutions to folks who need comfort objects at night. From this example, you could invite students to think about questions like "What could I design or create to support folks who still sleep with blankets or teddy bears even in adulthood?" Intriguing stories and facts spark the kind of curiosity that can lead to revolutionary thinking.

Curiosity Hardly Killed the Cat

We need students to know and understand that curiosity is a skill we truly desire to develop in them. We should want students to know that their questions are important to us. If we take the time to nurture our students' sense of curiosity, we are handing them the ability to shape the future for themselves. Great educators step away from thinking that developing a sense of curiosity in students is unnecessary and unrelated to great teaching. Instead, great educators know that curious minds can lead to lifesaving, world-changing solutions and that

1   "Third of Adults Still Sleep with 'Comfort Object' from Childhood, Survey Shows," Study Finds, June 12, 2019, https://www.studyfinds.org/third-adults-sleep-comfort-object -childhood/.

there is no greater place to unleash those minds than right inside our classrooms!

CURIOUS MINDS CAN LEAD TO LIFESAVING, WORLD-CHANGING SOLUTIONS.

HOPE

As adults, we understand the value of a hopeful attitude—that only with hope can we rise above difficult circumstances. Without hope, we can feel eternally trapped in despair. Our young people must also come to understand the power hope holds: its ability to help us heal, to grow, and to overcome what might seem like insurmountable experiences, all because inside we told ourselves things were going to be okay. By fostering a sense of hope, students will be able to see a light at the end of every tunnel and the joy that comes from never giving up even in the most difficult of times.

The Promise of a Better Future

Often students come to us carrying so many burdens. For some, their family lives may be horrendous. They may be troubled by their own social lives, or lack thereof. Their academic performance could have them feeling inadequate or as if they are not capable of measuring up to their more successful peers. And don't forget the perils of the world that may be plaguing them—political division tearing their families apart, fear of climate crisis, civil unrest, social injustices, and at the time I'm writing this, the threat of pandemic disease robbing them of their loved ones. Students may seem okay on the outside, but at any given moment, we could ask any of our students what is bothering them and they would most likely reply with a list of things weighing heavily on their minds. This is exactly why the promise of hope is essential to our students' understanding that with each new day they inch a little bit closer to a different and better future.

In classrooms where hope is abundant, students are happier, self-sufficient, confident, and goal oriented. As we design learning, taking steps to allow students to examine their hopes and to reflect on obstacles that may get in the way of learning is critical to their growth and success. We want our students to feel as if they are capable of persevering even in challenging situations and to understand that hope is a key mechanism behind that perseverance. But we cannot simply stop at teaching students about the meaning of hope and its power. We also need to show students that overcoming difficulty requires action, the ability to initiate the movement necessary to lead themselves toward a more desirable existence, now and in the future.

CHART the Way to Hope

Discuss hope and hopefulness often. Engage students in discussions surrounding the power of a hopeful spirit. Show them real-world examples of how hope has led others to fulfill their dreams and goals. As you engage them in learning, ask how hope affected the characters and real-life people they learned about in the content. Like other elements of CHARTing a course to a better world, we should model hope for our students by displaying our own hopeful mindset. Together, discuss with them how a sense of hope can hold the keys to both success and happiness in every part of their lives. Within your lessons, include exploration of figures who are known for being hopeful so that students have examples to follow when it comes to taking action toward reaching their goals and dreams.

Have students keep a goals and dreams journal. But don't just stop at having them write about the things they hope for. In their journals, encourage and support them in defining their plans to achieve those goals. Students need to understand that the path to meeting their goals requires a clear plan of action. Guide them in exploring the kinds of setbacks they may experience and what they can do to overcome them. Have students list the steps necessary to reach the small goals that will lead them toward the big ones. Discuss goals and dreams together to build a sense of community and belonging. Don't forget to celebrate even the smallest of achievements. This will go far in reinforcing the power of hope and its impact on their individual and collective lives.

Teach students the value of self-efficacy. Many of our students don't have folks at home (or elsewhere) talking with them about their goals, their hopes and dreams, let alone rooting them on or encouraging them that their dreams are possible. If students feel others don't believe in them, they may have a difficult time maintaining the sense of hope necessary to help them reach any kind of goal. We have to be our students' champions in this sense. If we set high expectations for students and provide them a path for fulfilling those expectations, we are in effect showing students that with focus and determination they can *and will* accomplish their goals. When we show students that we believe in them, they will also begin to believe in themselves, and will become confident, capable, goal-oriented, and hopeful individuals.

Hope Gives Way to Belief

In short, hope comes from our faith in accepting that things *will* be okay no matter how difficult times may be. To foster this acceptance, we must help our students develop the perseverance and determination to overcome the obstacles, setbacks, and challenges they will encounter as they endeavor to reach their goals. We must work with them to establish clear plans to reach those goals, but we must also encourage them to adopt action-oriented mindsets, because no matter how hopeful one is, dreams and goals can't be achieved without taking action to reach them. We must show students that we believe in them so they will believe in themselves. If we do these things, we provide them a chance at a future that is far more beautiful than they may have ever dreamed possible.

ADVOCACY

Helping students to understand the importance of advocacy is another area we must focus on as we design learning and classroom experiences for our students. In doing so, we equip them with the autonomy and determination to seek out answers and information as well as the confidence and courage necessary to create a desirable existence for themselves and others. Students who know how to advocate are able to help solve the problems that plague their own lives along with the complex and diverse ones that trouble the world.

The Mindset for Better Opportunity

The ability to self-advocate grants students access to the tools, resources, information, and supports they need to excel in life. If we don't teach self-advocacy, we risk releasing students into a sometimes unkind and unfair world that won't always have their best interests at heart. By learning to advocate for themselves, students can protect their educational and personal interests and learn to become good decision-makers. Students can and should learn to advocate for others, too.

Some students may never have been advised about the importance of advocating for themselves, let alone advocating on behalf of others. By encouraging students to approach societal issues and the lived experiences of others with a mindset centered on advocacy, we are teaching them to create a world in which everyone has a place, a voice, and a future. Through advocacy, we are teaching students that fairness and equality are fundamental elements of a society that is large enough for all people to coexist peacefully. Allowing students to explore ways in which they can respectfully and safely learn to advocate for the improved conditions of others, in the end, will make them better parents, better bosses, better friends, and overall, better people.

CHART the Way to Advocacy

Encourage awareness and knowing when to reach out for help. As educators, we know students often fail to ask those very important questions swirling around in their heads: *When was that assignment due? What resource did the teacher say to use? Where is that information we are supposed to reference?* Instead, some sit silently confused, or they utter that famous statement teachers love to hear: "I don't know what I am supposed to do." The real issue is, many students don't know *how* or *what* to ask when they are confused. The next time you see a perplexed face or you get hit with an "I'm confused" after assigning a task, have them complete sentence starters such as: *I think I need . . . , I'm having trouble with . . . ,* or *I don't know where to find . . .* Once they have their statements written down, open the floor for help. Encourage students to seek assistance from their peers or a trusted friend. Help them understand that practice translates into confidence and courage, and while they want to do their best to work problems out on their own, it's okay to ask for help, too. Encourage extremely shy students to communicate on paper or via email if that's easier for them.

Engage students in challenging conversations. While some educators may want to shy away from hot topics, great teachers resist the inclination to do so. One of the most important things we can do in our classrooms is give students a space to examine the issues and problems that currently affect society. For example, if you are taking active steps to weave antiracism education into your curriculum, challenging conversations are an important piece to include in your practice. As you build out antiracist learning opportunities, find ways to include topics that reveal the impacts of individual and systemic racism into your conversations. Our goal in bringing students to race-related conversations is to help them understand that some issues may have life-or-death implications for certain individuals based on the color of their skin. Regardless of your specific focus, however, take time to explore headlines with students, or have them brainstorm topics they know are controversial. Let them talk about why it is in fact important for them to understand these issues and how what they learn may someday help them offer up solutions to these problems. We cannot expect to develop passionate, advocacy-centered minds if we never expose students to the problems they don't yet know exist.

Allow students time to reflect. It's true that many of our students are not exposed to current social issues for any number of reasons: lack of access to media and information, general lack of interest or concern at home, or perhaps they simply live a sheltered life. Whatever the reason, introducing students to societal issues and problems will mean they need time for some introspection. Whether this comes in the form of giving students time to journal about their own thoughts and feelings or time to engage in reflective discussion as a group, we must grant students the opportunity to explore their own thought processes and emotions in some way. When we dedicate time for students to think deeply and reflectively about the issues that affect society, they will gain an understanding of how learning to advocate for others has the power to change the world for the better.

Advocacy Is Key to Empowerment

Empowering students with awareness and the capability to problem-solve can lead them to achieve what they never imagined was possible. Something as simple as gaining the courage to ask questions in English class may help to increase a student's confidence when questioning unjust actions outside of class. The feeling a student may get by speaking up, either for themselves or for someone else, may drive them to consider a career they never before saw themselves doing. Advocacy is at the heart of a just society, and individuals who possess strong advocacy skills are essential to helping improve it.

When designing learning experiences for our students, we must consider how we can include a focus on building advocacy skills. It's a task that requires a plan, but it most definitely *can* be done. We must simply be willing to do it. Great teachers know that great teaching is difficult, and they will never accept teaching in a classroom that does not include helping students to understand the power of advocacy.

WE CAN'T CHART OUR COURSE WITHOUT COLLABORATION

Creating a culture that embraces collaboration is vital to developing empathy and understanding in the classroom. Through the social interactions students experience when collaborating, we can teach them to have patience, to listen to and hear the voices of their peers, and to embrace the ideas and thinking of others. Students who know how to collaborate will be more effective as adults when they are required to work together to find ways of improving the world. Support students in their growth by doing things like shifting them around often so they sit near every student in the classroom at some point throughout the year and by making sure you give them the chance to problem-solve together regularly. Collaboration is a wonderful way to foster curiosity, hope, and advocacy.

RESPONSIBILITY

When we think of teaching students about the importance of responsibility, words like *accountability*, *honesty*, *self-motivation*, and *courage* probably come to mind. Traits like these are essential to students feeling good about themselves and to helping them understand the important role that responsibility plays in their being able to lead happy, successful lives. A sense of responsibility equates to doing the right thing and doing what you should do even when the situation is tough. Showing students how to have the courage to demonstrate responsibility when it is time can have a profound impact on their lives—and on the world, too.

The Behavior for a Better Society

Responsible students thrive, in the classroom and out. They accept their mistakes, and when they have missed the mark on something, they can take steps to rectify the situation. Whether it's missing an assignment deadline, treating someone with disrespect, or not living up to their word, responsible students know what it means to be accountable when they fall short of expectations, be it ours, theirs, or others'. The behavior of responsible citizens determines the kind of society we ultimately find ourselves living in. When individuals embrace a sense of responsibility, it allows all of us to feel safe and valued and to trust that those around us know how to make the right decisions for the good of everyone. We should create time to talk with students about these things.

Tailoring learning that allows students to make connections between responsibility and the overall improvement of society is a valuable step in our practice that we cannot overlook. Students face decision-making every day that can affect their lives and others'; therefore, we must embed opportunities to teach them how to exhibit responsible behavior. When we create learning that gives students the chance to show accountability and honesty, we are doing more than helping them develop skills. We are giving them the guidance to be able to leave our classrooms and make a lasting impression on the world they will someday work hard to improve. We have to show them that responsible individuals are reliable friends, trustworthy partners, and exceptional employees and that responsible people love themselves because they are proud of who they are. That, in its own special way, is a gift to society, too.

CHART the Way to Responsibility

Examine courageous behavior. Take time to discuss the actions of courageous individuals who felt they had a personal responsibility to act for the greater good of others. Introduce them to people like Rosa Parks, Gandhi, and Helen Keller. But also show them examples of young people whose courage has impacted the world. For instance, talk to them about individuals like David Hogg, a student survivor of the Marjory Stoneman Douglas High School shooting turned activist, who has helped lead high-profile protests and marches across America in support of gun reform. Or Malala Yousafzai, the Pakistani youth who was nearly assassinated for speaking out against the prohibition of the education of girls. Explain how Malala's social activism earned her the Nobel Prize for Peace in recognition of her efforts on behalf of children's rights. Because these may seem like extraordinary acts of courage, allow students to explore how their own individual actions, no matter how small, might have positively impacted an outcome. Have them write and share stories of times when they felt empowered by their sense of personal responsibility to act courageously. Learning from each other's successes will help students gain the confidence to do the right thing the next time they find themselves in a challenging situation.

Let students make the rules and the consequences. At the beginning of the school year, take the opportunity to infuse the discussion of personal and social responsibility into your process by democratically establishing rules and consequences for classroom behavior. Allow students time to brainstorm ideas for classroom policy surrounding how our actions foster or inhibit a sense of responsibility. Also have students discuss logical and realistic consequences that will improve the overall culture and climate of the classroom. Include topics like honesty, accountability, and self-motivation in your planning session. If students aren't familiar with how these topics affect our ability to "do the right thing," this is a great place to open that discussion. As students suggest ideas for rules, have them provide insight on how those rules will help them develop a sense of responsibility to ourselves and others, and what should happen when we don't act in responsible ways. Make sure students understand that the rules and consequences they develop are less about enforcing compliance and more about helping them gain the skills that will help them be successful later in life.

Focus on media literacy and communication. Each day, students find themselves engulfed by social media, so determining when and how to respond to what they see, hear, or read is a critical skill for them. Social responsibility, taking other peoples' feelings, interests, and needs into account, is equally as important as personal responsibility. Especially as it pertains to social media, students need to understand that their actions may have the potential to harm others. Any chance you get, give students the opportunity to engage in developing both media literacy and communication skills. Help them learn to decode media messaging and engage them in how to properly construct their own media or how to respond to others' so that what they communicate is acceptable, appropriate, and helpful, *not* hurtful. Encouraging them to pause and reflect will help students in making the right decisions before posting on social media or responding reactively to something online. Help them practice this valuable skill by presenting "How Would You Respond?" scenarios that require students to work together to decide upon responsible actions related to what they see in the media. These could include sample social media posts, videos, even fake news or other unreliable online media. Be sure to include time for debrief and reflection, as these are critical to helping students process their learning.

It's the Greatest Gift We Can Give

By the end of each school year, every one of our students should be able to identify the tenets that represent and the actions that display both personal and social responsibility. We should want our students to understand what responsibility is in every sense of the word: to be able to recognize it when they see it and, most importantly, to know how to show it. Just as with curiosity, hope, and advocacy, we may be the only ones who ever help our students learn this valuable skill. Giving them access to the kind of learning that helps them grow into responsible citizens who are accountable, trustworthy, and courageous is a gift that will benefit them their entire lives—one they will also be able to pass on to others someday.

TOLERANCE

Whenever possible, we should plan to expose students to diversity and to model for students what it means to display tolerance. Doing so will help students develop the behaviors and attitudes that strengthen society and will allow them to connect with others in ways they never imagined they could. Exploring tolerance takes courage and deliberate action on the part of educators. We may have to bring students to uncomfortable conversations, but that is something you'll have to get comfortable with yourself if you want to teach students to embrace a world filled with diversity and individualism. Before anything else, however, we need to ensure students fully understand the meaning of the word *tolerance.*

When I first ask students what tolerance means, a good majority of them are not able to articulate an entirely accurate definition of the word. They immediately associate the word with its relative *tolerate*, rendering a definition that sounds a bit like "to put up with something." I quickly engage them in a contest to see who can locate the correct definition of *tolerance* by asking them to use their devices to find the dictionary definition of the word—a competitive activity that we engage in often. Believe me, most middle- and high-schoolers love a good challenge!

After a few contributions, one persistent youngster usually delivers us the definition we are looking for: "Sympathy or indulgence for beliefs or practices differing from or conflicting with one's own." We explore this idea a bit further by analyzing the definition of the word as shared in UNESCO's Declaration of Principles on Tolerance:

> Tolerance is respect, acceptance and appreciation of the rich
> diversity of our world's cultures, our forms of expression

and ways of being human. . . . Tolerance is harmony in difference.[2]

We investigate how this definition is different from *tolerate* by further analyzing the words that make up the meaning of *tolerance*: sympathy, respect, acceptance, diversity. After some discussion, it's clear that folks who exhibit tolerance are those who desire to understand, accept, and embrace others for who they are. We wrap up with a quick reflection on how an attitude of tolerance might improve our classroom, our lives, and our journey through life.

The Heart for Better Relationships

Possessing an attitude of tolerance makes us better at not just understanding others but also understanding the impact that we have on others. Whether our students plan to be future teachers, doctors, CEOs, essential workers, or visionaries, they need to know how their attitudes and perspectives impact those they lead and serve. Becoming more tolerant makes us overall kinder, happier, healthier people, and who doesn't want to be those things?

The need to engage students in developing more tolerant attitudes may seem like a given. Just turn on the television and you won't have to search long to determine that the world could use a whole lot more empathy. Hate and intolerance seem to be everywhere we look, yet many turn a blind eye to issues they feel don't affect them. However, if making the world a better place isn't a good enough reason to help students become more compassionate people, then how about the fact that one's sense of tolerance can have a profound impact on their success in life, specifically as it relates to building relationships with others.

CHART the Way to Tolerance

Focus on building relationships and culture, above all else. We know that a strong classroom culture is critical to learning, but it also has

---

2   United Nations Educational, Scientific, and Cultural Organization (UNESCO), *Declaration of Principles on Tolerance*, UNESCO General Session 28, Paris, November 16, 1995.

an impact on the attitudes of our students toward one another. We must regularly find time to allow students to engage with each other in ways that allow them to learn about their peers. Provide opportunities for students to complete activities that incorporate their passions, interests, family lives, goals, and dreams. These things can be easily integrated into projects, essays, performance-based assessments, and more. But don't stop there. We have to allow students to share these experiences with one another. Allowing them to present, peer edit, or post their work on social media gives students direct access to each other's lives. In doing this, students are able to see the similarities between themselves and others, strengthening both the culture of the classroom and the relationships within it.

Design a classroom that speaks the language of tolerance. As we seek to develop tolerant mindsets in our students, it's important to begin by examining what our own classroom says about tolerance. Review what is on your classroom walls. What messages are present? Do they represent the collective body of your student population, and is that adequate? How does your own personal attitude toward tolerance prevail, from what you wear to the words you speak to the visual messaging you share? How do students know from the way you have created your own classroom that tolerance is a quality you embrace? Like everything else, we must show students that we practice what we preach.

Facilitate learning through the lenses of others. When engaging students in learning, consider the role empathy plays within our content areas. In literature, we might discuss with students how outcomes could have been different if certain characters had better related with one another. When we help students see alternate pathways to problem-solving, we also help them see the value in all their peers' contributions. When giving students the chance to talk about their personal lives, include the opportunity to discuss how empathy, or the lack thereof, has impacted them or their loved ones. Ask students if they feel understood or if they feel they understand others. When we planning for instruction, collaboration, and discussion, we should find ways to include others' perspectives and feelings and ask students how knowing these things affected their learning. We should seek to immerse students in learning environments that allow them to learn from one another in the context of their differing perspectives.

Reflection Is Critical to Understanding

While these strategies will help students develop tolerance, we cannot forget to reflect on how students' attitudes have been shaped by their experiences and interactions with others in the classroom. We need to ask students to think about how the space in which they learn has helped them become more accepting of others. We should ask students how collaboration has improved their ability to work with others. Invite students to compare their perspectives with those of the voices you have invited into your learning environment. Developing tolerance for others and embracing diversity involves some introspection, and we need to allow time for students to process what they have experienced. This opportunity for reflection is critical to understanding the difference between students feeling like they have an obligation to put up with someone versus the need (and the desire) to embrace the diversity that surrounds them.

Foster Antiracism and Tolerance Using the Voices of Many

You may be familiar with the African proverb "It takes a village to raise a child." This proverb implies that an entire community of people must interact with children for those children to experience and grow in a safe and healthy environment. I wholeheartedly agree with the sentiment of this beautiful proverb, but with a minor revision: that village must be intentionally designed so that it fosters antiracism and tolerance in every way. As educators, administrators, and others responsible for the education of children, we must find ways to transform classrooms into villages filled with diverse voices—and not just voices that come from within our content, but that come from the front of the room as well. You can do this in a few simple steps:

1. **Find those willing to join you in conversations about race within your school.** Your task will be much easier and much less scary if you don't have to do it on your own. Form an anti-racism PLC inside your school consisting of educators who are willing to interject multicultural perspectives into the content they teach. Plan to reference other educators' content in your own instruction, mentioning what those teachers are discussing in their classrooms. Extend their conversations into your own by allowing students to lead with what they have learned.

2. **Step outside your school to find those whose stories bring awareness.** Bring voices from a range of career fields, from different cultures, different locations, different ethnic backgrounds, who can provide students with new perspectives. Think about when and how you can invite parents, caregivers, or family members into your classroom to share their stories or messages. Reach out to your local pastors, business owners, and district leaders to see if they might be willing to talk to your students.

3. **Partner with universities for opportunities to mentor preservice teachers.** Preservice teachers make great coteaching partners in the classroom, and this practice allows you to speak as a unified voice in front of children. Conversely, you can show students how to respectfully agree to disagree on topics. Either way, coteaching is a terrific way to tackle tough topics like racism.

4. **Connect with your professional learning network (PLN).** Very different from your PLC, your PLN is your "squad." They have your back, and they will be there to help you when you need

it. Invite them to Zoom with your students. Connect your classrooms, especially those that are demographically different from one another. We live in a digital age. There is nothing we can't do via the power of technology.

Whether you work in a diverse school district or not, there are many ways you can build alliances and design a village that will help you educate every child you serve. When we do this for our students—when we let them learn from *many* voices—we are offering them new perspectives that might be exactly what they need to help them grab on to empathy.

I know this sounds challenging, but with some intentionality and a little PIRATE planning, this can be done even in the least diverse communities. We have a responsibility, and the time is now. So, go, build that village!

Through a careful design for learning, we *can* connect curiosity, hope, advocacy, responsibility, and tolerance to all we do in our classrooms. We should always strive for our teaching practice to be impactful, but as great educators we also want to touch our students' hearts and bring them to understanding that extends beyond our content. We should seek, in every way, to invite our students into learning environments that offer them a glimpse at a better world and that create in them an "anything is possible" mindset. CHARTing the course to a better world is the foundation for *beyond-great* teaching. Make this a priority, and you'll change far more than students' lives; you'll be shaping the future of our world.

DROP ANCHOR

- In what ways do you model and encourage advocacy or curiosity within the context of the learning experiences that you create for your students?
- Throughout the school year, how will you continue to foster and exhibit hope even when you may be struggling occasionally yourself?
- How do you engage your students in understanding the need for personal responsibility? In what ways do you offer them the opportunity to develop both social and personal responsibility skills?
- What are some strategies you currently use or would like to use to ensure your students understand what it means to demonstrate an attitude of tolerance?
- Make a list of people you could include in your intentionally designed village who will support you as you strive to create antiracist learning environments for students.
- Have a conversation with students about what it means to CHART a course to a better world and why this is a priority for you as a teacher. Invite students to provide their own input on how incorporating these elements into learning may help them beyond the day-to-day learning in your classroom.
- Reflect on why it's important for you personally to become the kind of educator who CHARTs a course to a better world right within your classroom. How will doing so help you and your students achieve greatness? What is at stake if we don't apply these elements to our everyday practice?

PART II

Plan It

DEEPEN YOUR PRACTICE

THREE

Build a Vessel for Student Engagement

Engagement isn't a thing. It's the only thing.
—CHRISTOPHER LEHMAN

*W*ouldn't it be wonderful if every student walked into our classrooms thirsty for knowledge and longing for us to light in them the spark that would set their minds on fire for learning? That would be amazing! But the fact of the matter is, few students come running into our classes ready to jump head first into learning. Instead, many of our students come to us hungry, tired, upset, scared, or even sick, and the last thing on their minds is what we have prepared to teach them on any given day.

We have high hopes for our students. We think that if we could only get their full attention or help them discover their passion for learning, they would learn to see the value of school and education. Of course, we want these things for students. We want to see them excel in every way, but the reality is that there are obstacles we need to help students overcome before they are actually *able* to find themselves in love with learning. Another very important part of planning for student success is to build a platform for engagement that enables students to invest themselves fully in the learning we've worked so hard to design for them.

CHIEF ENGAGEMENT OFFICERS

I like to think of our primary role in the classroom as that of CEO: *chief engagement officer.* When students arrive with what some might refer to as "baggage," the task of engaging students in the act of learning can often seem insurmountable. Some of our kiddos may not particularly enjoy our content, or they may feel incapable of success in an area and, therefore, be inclined to check out. Some may have other stressors in their lives impeding their ability to focus on anything other than their own personal problems. It is our responsibility to acknowledge this and to figure out, despite students' individual obstacles to learning, how we can bring them to a love of learning, no matter the topic or venue.

As successful CEOs, we must be consistently focused on creating a clear path to engagement for all students. This begins with helping them to develop a sense of curiosity and wonder about what they will learn while they are with us and by removing any barriers that might get in the way of learning. We must accept and embrace pausing to regroup and the act of reflection as essential classroom practices. And if we ask students to come to us with an empty cup eager to be filled, then we must reciprocate with a commitment to crafting engaging learning experiences that not only meet them where they are but also generate a sense of excitement about learning that keeps them on their toes. Our success as CEOs relies heavily on our ability to do these things.

LAUNCH LEARNING WITH WONDERINGS

The questions we engage students in exploring at the start of any new lesson should serve to spark curiosity and establish relevance so that students will see the necessity of what they are learning and invest themselves in the new information we are about to share with them. These moments at the outset have the power to transform our classroom environment as well as students' mindsets by helping them to see value in our content.

Inspired by ideas presented by Connie Moss and Susan Brookhart in their book *Learning Targets*,[1] I begin new learning segments with Wonderings, a three-pronged discussion that assists students in exploring why the lesson will be important to them and to their individual success. These questions guide our brief introductory conversation:

1. What is the learning about, and why does it matter?
2. What will you do with this new information?
3. How will this learning help you in your life?

This opening dialogue helps students tie the forthcoming knowledge and associated skills to the real world and to their own lives, and is critical in showing students how the material can be shaped into and used for something that matters to them. It also helps to resolve that famous question teachers often get from students: *When am I ever going to use this?* The most wonderful thing is, students' answers are usually unique to each and every one of them.

Wondering #1: What is the learning about, and why does it matter?

At the outset of a new unit or lesson, you are asking students to invest their time in something entirely new. Students need to be granted time to explore why they should make such an investment. Think for a moment about any telemarketing call you've ever gotten. If the caller is savvy enough to have kept you on the phone longer than ten seconds, the next questions out of your mouth are "What is this all about?" and "How is this going to help or benefit me?" Like those annoying but

---

1 Connie M. Moss and Susan M. Brookhart, *Learning Targets: Helping Students Aim for Understanding in Today's Lesson* (Alexandria, VA: Association for Supervision and Curriculum Development, 2012).

skilled callers, educators must immediately engage students in discovering why this new learning is worth their time.

Wondering #1 asks students to simply consider why this learning matters and involves asking two additional questions:

- I wonder where this kind of knowledge might be useful or who might use this kind of information or skill set.
- To what end might this knowledge or these skills be used?

A word of caution: While beginning new learning with student-friendly "I can" statements is fine, I do not like to muddy up our Wonderings with standards-based language. Doing so can negate the effects of this process. Our goal is to help students truly engage in understanding why a topic such as the one we are about to learn is important *beyond* its being a part of the content and the standards we are required to cover in the class. For example, in eighth-grade English language arts we might post the standards-based "I can" on our classroom wall for reference: "I can identify how certain word choices influence the meaning and tone of a text." Our Wondering session might briefly reference this statement; however, our conversation will shed light on how our ability to choose words can have a profound effect on our interactions with others and how what they are about to learn might help them become better at choosing their words. Our conversation should reveal to students that they are learning this skill not because the standards for their grade level say they should, but because it is going to improve their lives in some way.

Wondering #2: What will you do with this new information?

We should begin engaging students in deeper-level thinking early in a new unit or lesson, or even at its outset. This next step in the Wondering process does just that, as it involves students in a discussion about how they might be able to demonstrate mastery and understanding of new learning.

At this point, we can start to share with students the kinds of assessments they will be exposed to in the unit. This includes both formative assessments within individual lessons and final summative assessments that will allow them to show mastery of the concepts and skills we explore together. Our role in this exercise is nothing more than to facilitate the discussion surrounding how these assessments can help them grow.

After you reveal the kinds of assessments students will be engaged in, ask students to begin thinking about how the assessments they encounter might be modified to meet their needs. If you are running a student-centered learning environment, this should be something students are experienced in doing. If not, you'll need to think about whether the assessments you have designed allow students flexibility in demonstrating mastery and make any necessary revisions. You'll also want to provide students with an understanding of the criteria for measuring success and performing quality work, with your own understanding that each student has different goals and objectives based on their learning needs. In this part of the discussion, engage students in questions like

- What else might they be able to do with this new knowledge or information?
- How might they be able to demonstrate their own understanding beyond completion of the assessments you provide to them?
- Which of their own strengths will be an asset to them while they are learning this?

We must be prepared to ask students to bring their strengths to new learning in order to capitalize on them. We need to help students understand that a new lesson doesn't mean they are going in cold. They already have knowledge and skills that will set them up for success. For example, in a learning segment where students are exploring characters in Greek mythology, students may be asked to create a family tree that captures all of the major players in the stories they read together. Students' confidence and engagement will increase as they are asked to consider that they may be very good at organizing things or that they are great at picking out details that could help them make sense of new information they acquire.

Wondering #3: How will this learning help you in your life?

Step three of the Wonderings discussion is where students get to see how the learning connects to their own lives and how it has the potential to shape what they do in other classes and throughout their future. In this short but meaningful step, students will think about their own future—their interests, hopes, and dreams—and make connections between the new learning and its relevance to their own lives. The prompt is simply this:

- Now or in the future, this knowledge and/or these skills might be able to help me . . .

Here, we will engage students in the process of thinking about other classes in which they might use this skill; where in their lives they may already find themselves doing things that involve this information or competency; or how their future hopes, dreams, and goals rest upon having the expertise or understanding they are about to develop here.

∼

The entire Wonderings process may be brief if we are talking about a shorter learning segment, or it could be lengthier based on the complexity of the learning or the prior experience students have had with similar learning. It should also be said that this process is not designed to be a daily or even weekly practice, but rather should be used when students will be engaged in learning segments that are being introduced for the first time.

It should go without saying that inviting students to engage in Wonderings about new learning requires us as CEOs to have a clear plan for said learning before we even think about beginning this process. We must have created a path from learning target to strategically designed assessment so that the learning we engage students in and the assessments we provide along the way come as no surprise to them. Not taking the steps to carefully craft learning pathways in advance of taking students through these Wonderings is the first step to losing students in the process of educating them.

REMOVE BARRIERS BY BROADENING ACCESS TO INFORMATION

The inability to find information and communicate effectively are two of the biggest challenges our students face when it comes to being successful in the classroom. We can empower students by improving the ways in which we provide access to information that supports learning and by helping them learn to communicate so they are able to become better self-advocates. When students understand how and where to get information and can communicate with us when they can't, they are set free from the stress of "not knowing." A significant portion of this burden rests with educators, in that as we create the learning, we must be sure we have provided the kinds of resources and supports that will guide students to success.

Design Information Docks

Whether it's in your physical classroom or a digital classroom space, create a one-stop shop where students can find any and all information they need to be successful in your class: classroom codes, expectations, calendars, online links, anything that you will use day to day for learning. Replicate your dock on your syllabus or classroom information sheet to help support students (and parents) with accessing the resources when they are at home. Reserve space for important classroom account information, email and contact information, your social media handles, and any other relevant details that will be helpful to students and their families. You will be giving parents and students quick access to the information and everyday resources they need whether they are inside or outside of class and will free them from having to go through who knows what to find what it is they are looking for!

Categorize Assignments by Units or Topics

Whether you're using Google, Microsoft, or any other online learning management system, it's important that students can easily find what they need. I like to label shared folders and online notebooks by the titles of our units of study. If you have your own website, categorize important links and resources by topics or units, too. Labeling by dates or weeks can be confusing for students as it is easy to lose track of where we are on the schedule, especially considering some students might get behind due to absences, and there is often a need to adjust our calendars due to shifts in the direction of our instruction or other unforeseen circumstances. Categorizing assignments makes finding materials much easier for you and for students. Once you have decided upon the topic of your lesson or unit, you can then group all items together in the same place. If I give paper handouts for anything at all, I label them the same so students know that particular document is part of the unit, too.

Encourage Students to Use Online Calendars to Track What's Due

When it's time to turn in an assignment, how often have you heard your students say, "I didn't know that was due"? I know I sure have heard it a lot! Thankfully, helping your students learn to utilize online calendars to track their assignments will eliminate a lot of confusion regarding when an assignment needs to be submitted to you for feedback. Make sure students know how and where to access their calendars and how to set reminders if the system you utilize is not automatically set up to do so. In Google Classroom, for example, students can easily see what's due by accessing their Google Calendar from the "Classwork" tab. By clicking the calendar icon at the top of the tab, the calendar will open and students will be able to see all assignments for that class right before their eyes. They can change the view to be able to see a day, week, or month at a time.

Allow Students to Use Various Communication Methods

It's completely up to you, but I like to give students a number of methods for communicating with me. I have students who contact me with questions using the Remind app, a safe two-way messaging platform built for educators. Some students like to communicate via email, while others like to message me in a Google Chat. I'm open to this because, as an adult, I use various methods for communicating with others myself—depending on where I am, what I need to communicate, and who I am communicating with, I might use Facebook Messenger, WhatsApp, Voxer (a walkie-talkie app for team communication), or plain, old text messaging to connect. Students should also have access to multiple communication tools. The manner in which you choose to engage in communication with students is a decision you will have to make on your own, as you will be the one responding. You may want to try out different platforms to see what works best, and your students may even offer suggestions or ideas. Regardless, the goal is clear, easy, safe, and responsive communication to help students get the information they need quickly and easily so they remain engaged in learning! Be sure to share your preferred methods with students' family members and caregivers. They'll be glad to know they have options when reaching out to you as well.

Teach Students the Fine Art of Email Communication

If you have ever gotten an email from a student, you know what a treat that can be! I've seen subject lines that are questions or even miniparagraphs: "i'm going to be out of school tomorrow what am I going to miss," or "I turned in my assignment." While the communication and follow-up is appreciated, we are not doing students (or ourselves!) any favors if we don't help them learn to communicate more effectively via email.

Take time to go over email etiquette with students. Explain what each part of the email composition window is for and what it means. These are life skills that will help them improve their communication and self-advocacy, and you might just save your own sanity as well! Have students practice sending emails to one another. Remember, some students may never have learned anything about letter writing. Creating a few short lessons to practice this skill will go a long way.

Overcoming Obstacles in Creating Antiracist Learning Environments

Approaching the planning of antiracist teaching and learning with the mindset that we won't encounter setbacks is both naive and dangerous. We have to be prepared as much as possible to deal with the trials that come along with our task. Here are a few things to consider as you work to transform your classroom.

Define Your Mission

Take time, in advance of planning, to develop your overall mission or goal as it pertains to antiracism education and engaging students in learning about antiracism. This preparation will help you to remain steadfast and focused on the kind of change you have the power to bring about in doing antiracist work in your classroom.

Consider the Demographic of Your Classroom

The demographics of your classroom or school may have an impact on how you approach antiracism education with students. Consider these as you develop antiracism learning activities for any age or group. It's important to understand who your students are before you attempt to teach *them* about their own lived experiences and the struggles *they* face.

Learn about Your Students' Awareness of Racism

Learn more about your students' current views surrounding equity, race, and racism by using surveys, discussions, or writing prompts. Knowing where your students stand on these issues will aid you in developing learning activities that build students up as opposed to tearing them down.

Be Prepared to Deal with Challenging Questions

Many students will ask tough but honest questions when you begin to dig into antiracism education. Be prepared to handle those questions by thinking about what students might ask or be curious about ahead of time. If you don't have answers for them, it's okay. Let students know you are learning with them. Honesty goes a long way with kids!

Understand the Effects of Your Own Race as an Educator

Your own race can have a significant impact on how students receive your messaging about antiracism. You must consider how what you say in the color of your own skin affects students' thinking. You have the power to evoke positive change or to perpetuate negative attitudes and actions.

Anticipate Differences in Thinking between You and Your Students

Educators' belief systems are sometimes very different than those of their students. When talking about equity and antiracism with young people, you must be careful not to devalue their culture or belief systems, but instead help them construct new ideas about their previous ways of thinking.

ALLOW TIME TO PAUSE AND REFLECT

When it comes to managing and supporting students' social-emotional and mental health, educators have a challenging job. We must continually have our finger on the pulse of our classroom, looking and listening for those situations that require us to take a moment from whatever we are doing to pause. I cannot emphasize enough how important this is. We must always pay attention to what our students are saying, what they are doing, and how they are responding in any given situation, academic or otherwise. We might observe students responding to stressors stemming from inside or outside the classroom. We might have a single student experiencing difficulty, or it could be the entire class. Our students could be struggling based on something we said, did, or taught, or they could be feeling the stress of a current event or social issue that affects them or others they care about.

WE MUST CONTINUALLY HAVE OUR FINGER ON THE PULSE OF OUR CLASSROOM

Regardless of the cause, it is our job to identify when these situations arise. Students who are feeling stressed in the classroom are not going to digest the content we put in front of them, no matter what it is. Listen to your inner teacher voice and recognize when your students need to take time to pause, regroup, and reflect. Ask yourself or your students what they need: a conversation, a celebration, or a full-on cessation to address a situation. The fact of the matter is, we can't keep trudging forward if our kiddos have checked out, emotionally or physically. Together, we need to get to the root of the issue and allow students the time they need to get back on track.

PLAN OUTSIDE-THE-BOX EXPERIENCES

With the arrival of the COVID-19 pandemic, teachers around the world went to unimaginable extremes to find ways to engage students in educational settings that ranged from fully online learning environments to hybrid mixes of online and traditional classrooms. Yes, these kinds of educational environments did already exist; however, many of the traditional brick-and-mortar schools upended by the pandemic were not prepared to make the shift in terms of technology infrastructure or pedagogical approach to teaching and learning online. Further, parents and students now had to share the same spaces in the home for both work and learning, while parents and caregivers became teacher aides during bouts of remote learning. Teachers and students who were still learning in person faced round after round of quarantined students who struggled to remain caught up at school. But none of this stopped teachers from becoming superheroes who saved the day—and probably the whole dang planet!

Uncertain times pushed educators' abilities to engage students into unfamiliar territory. Strategies and teaching methods that had worked before could no longer be relied upon. Despite all this, educators and administrators worked hard to ensure students still had access to technology, food, counseling, and other vital supports. Equally important, they had to make sure students were receiving a high-quality education, despite the method of delivery. And teachers would not allow for anything less. They were committed to doing whatever it took to ensure students got the education that was rightfully theirs. What educators were able to do together in those challenging times to meet the needs of our learners was remarkable. If we could make these kinds of adjustments to engage students during a pandemic, we can and should continue that shift in thinking about how we engage students beyond it.

That said, it should remain the goal of educators to focus on planning outside-the-box learning experiences for our students. There is no shortage of strategies, methods, or information to help us create learning environments that students will want to run into instead of away from, as Beth Houf and Shelley Burgess, authors of *Lead Like A PIRATE*, would say. We now have more access to free professional development and free classroom technology than ever before. Continuing their commitment to outside-the-box teaching for the sake of kids, great teachers will go to great lengths to engage every learner. The ways in which we can do this *really are* limitless. Here are just a few:

Find new pals online. Connect your classroom with others. There are plenty of teachers both inside and outside your own building who would be willing to collaborate with you and your classes. You could read and analyze a book together, work on collaborative projects, or simply become pen pals. Use platforms like Zoom, Flipgrid, or Google Meet to bring students face-to-face in the virtual world to learn and grow together.

Explore passions. Allow students time to examine the things they are most passionate about. Use online curation tools like Wakelet or Padlet as mediums for creating and presenting passion projects. These performance-based assessments allow students to engage in inquiry-based service learning where students can embed content-area learning into student-centered projects. Give students access to other web-based platforms like Weebly or Google Sites that allow them to include internet links, images, video recordings, and more to enhance the interactive nature of their projects. Andi McNair's book *Genius Hour* is a great resource to learn more about how to implement passion projects into your curriculum.

Take learning outside. Go on a walking field trip, craft poetry on the sidewalk, have circle time or Socratic seminars in the grass. The possibilities for connecting learning with the outdoors are unlimited. Do be intentional, though. You are still planning a learning opportunity, and that means you have done the work ahead of time to make the outdoor experience successful. Kids will be grateful for these experiences and will have much to talk about for a long time to come.

Let students lead with their own questions. Teachers are continually asking students questions. For a change, let students come up with their own guiding questions. Beginning with an idea shared by Tara Martin, author of *Be REAL*, ask students to work through the formation of their own possibility questions surrounding a topic or skill you have presented to them in class. For example, when reading literature or exploring a new topic, give students question stems like the ones below and allow them to finish them with endings related to the material they have been studying:

- How might the protagonist have . . . ?
- In what ways could the author . . . ?
- How could readers connect . . . ?

This student-centered activity will allow students to engage with learning on a much deeper level, heightening engagement as students ask questions about content that matters to them. Give them the space to share their questions with others in the class and use those questions to spark discussion, plan writing assignments, or form assessment activities that will lead students to new understandings.

GREAT CEOS HELP LEARNERS SET SAIL

Every day that we walk into our classrooms, we find ourselves looking out at a sea of faces staring back at us, most likely wondering what new learning we have planned for them in that moment. As chief engagement officers, establishing a clear path for engagement and finding ways to help students overcome obstacles to learning are important to both our students' success and our own. Fortunately, there are countless ways in which we can move students beyond the traditional ways of "doing" school. Sticking to the same old ways of thinking when we plan learning experiences for our students is not only detrimental to your performance as an educator, but it robs students of the chance to develop a love for learning and may even prevent them from pushing themselves to learn new things. Great CEOs understand that their goal in all things is to provide students with the information, tools, and resources necessary to help them excel in any content area, in any setting, every single day.

DROP ANCHOR

✖ What strategies do you presently use to engage students? How might you adapt these to make them more "outside-the-box"? What steps do you take now to ensure that students see the value in what they are learning?

✖ Plan time in your schedule to revisit with students how and where they can find the information they need in order to be successful in your class. Make time to engage them in discussion about how they can communicate with you and also how they can find answers on their own. Remind them of the importance of self-advocacy.

✖ Revisit your syllabus. Analyze its effectiveness as a one-stop information shop that will provide students access to information and remove barriers to learning. Update whatever is necessary and redistribute it to students and parents. It's never too late to provide information to anyone!

✖ What steps are you taking currently to engage and grow your students within an antiracist learning environment? What obstacles do you still need to overcome in order to make this happen? How do you plan on overcoming them?

FOUR

Sailing the High, Deep, and Wide Seas of Differentiation

The teacher is an irreplaceable leader in moving differentiation from an idea on paper . . . to a way of life in the classroom.

—CAROL ANN TOMLINSON AND MARCIA IMBEAU

The best educators are those who provide students with opportunities to learn through inquiry and the exploration of big ideas. They engage each student in higher-order thinking as often as possible. However, when students arrive in our classrooms with different skill sets, varied interests and learning styles, or a range of ability levels, it can be challenging to craft learning that meets the needs of an entire classroom. The ability to differentiate effectively is a vital component of great teaching that doesn't happen accidentally. It happens because of darn good planning.

Whether we find ourselves teaching in self-contained classrooms, those in which students share similar academic requirements, or in fully inclusive learning environments, all students, regardless of their abilities, need to be offered tailored learning experiences and the opportunity to demonstrate mastery of their skills and an understanding of the complex ideas we present to them. And while planning with differentiation in mind can seem like a daunting task, with a few tweaks to the process, you'll soon find yourself skilled at designing learning that meets the developmental needs of every learner in your classroom. To help all students sail skillfully throughout their own learning journey, we have to plan high, plan deep, and plan wide.

PLANNING HIGH

Planning high means creating tiered learning targets, starting from the ability level of our highest-performing learners. This practice is not always easy for educators to embrace at first. We may feel intimidated by the idea of using our highest achievers as the baseline from which we build targets for lower-level performers, but it is a very strategic way of addressing the needs of all students. Setting the bar high means we leave room to modify goals to meet the needs of students who may struggle, because we can adjust entry and exit points for all learners, from top to bottom.

Later, when designing tiered assessments, lessons, and activities, we may need to spend a little more time building out learning plans on the front end. But on the back end—when it's time for kids to actually engage in learning—we will have time freed up for support during instruction and assessment.

Begin with the End in Mind

The first step in any new design for learning is to establish the rationale for teaching what it is that we plan to assess in the future—or to begin with the end in mind. This means before we identify a target or plan a single part of a learning segment, our task is to figure out what it is that students need to learn as well as how they will show us they have mastered it.

Beginning with the end in mind requires us to answer two questions:

- What do we want students to be able to do?

- How will students show us they know how to do it?

In their book, *Understanding by Design*, Grant Wiggins and Jay McTighe suggest three essential steps to designing solid learning plans for students:

1. "Identify desired results" by using informative data to determine learning targets.
2. "Determine acceptable evidence" by developing measurement and assessment tools to monitor student progress toward goals.
3. "Plan learning experiences and instruction" by filling in the gaps between assessments with tiered lessons.[1]

The basic concept that Wiggins and McTighe put forth is that planning should be done in a backward fashion. Too often, teachers want to begin instructional planning around a central topic, a resource, or even an idea. While these things can—and should—be included in the instructional-design process, they should not be alone at its center, nor should they be our first consideration in planning. Instead, when designing learning segments, teachers should open the exploration of learning topics by analyzing collected data that tells us who our students are, what they know, and *what they have the potential to achieve.*

Find the Entry Points

Before we begin to establish learning targets, we need to evaluate what our data says about what our students can and cannot do. This data can come from standardized assessments, diagnostic assessments, informative classroom assessments, or perhaps even some form of observation.

Often, educators begin planning learning by deciding to "teach" some skill or introduce some bit of knowledge without even knowing where students are with regard to said learning. When we do this, we are making an assumption that our students are all entering into

---

1   Grant P. Wiggins and Jay McTighe, *Understanding by Design* (Alexandria, VA: Association for Supervision and Curriculum Development, 2008).

learning at the same spot. But we know that simply isn't true. We don't approach learning with the mindset that all students possess the same knowledge and skills, so why would we begin planning that way?

Before we determine what it is we're going to ask students to do, we must first figure out what learning students need help with most.

Identify Learner Groups

Once we have determined how we want students to show mastery and have evaluated student data from an assessment, our next step is to disaggregate that data in order to group students according to their performance on the assessment. (Note: this grouping process is for the purposes of planning only and, for me, does not always correspond with students' physical arrangement or grouping for collaboration in the classroom.) This data analysis involves going beyond simply looking at a number or score our students earned. Analyzing the data in this case means we are looking beyond scores to determine where within the data set students are performing similarly. Key questions we might ask ourselves in completing our analysis include: What skills or traits align within certain groups of students? And where is there a clear distinction between the performance level or ability of one group and that of another?

For example, in eighth-grade social studies, data from one benchmark assessment might highlight areas for growth that align within subgroups regardless of the group's overall performance on the whole assessment. By first identifying the focus for growth of the learners with the highest ability in tier three, we can easily modify the instructional focus for the remaining students in tiers two and one by analyzing their assessment data, and then beginning the process of differentiating learning targets based on the identified needs within each tier. Consider this grouping, modified from the Common Core standards:

Tier 3–Students who cannot yet but will be able to:
- distinguish among fact, opinion, and reasoned judgment in a text
- identify key steps in a text's description of a process related to history/social studies

Tier 2–Students who cannot yet but will be able to:
- identify key steps in a text's description of a process related to history/social studies
- integrate visual information with other information in print and digital texts

Tier 1–Students who cannot yet but will be able to:
- integrate visual information with other information in print and digital texts[2]
- provide an accurate summary of a source distinct from prior knowledge or opinions

As you can see, the instructional focus of each group is adjusted into three separate but increasingly complex categories based on what the data says each student group cannot yet do. By analyzing more than the students' normative data or averages, we are able to clearly see a distinction between the ability levels of all our students, which leads us to ask ourselves where we go from here. We are certainly not going to build one learning target for the entire class around tier three, because where then would that leave our lowest-ability group? We will need to create multiple learning targets. This evaluative process is highly important if you wish to tailor learning to meet the needs of all learners so that you can focus on the various ways in which each child is able to demonstrate learning. This is the entire purpose of differentiation.

Carol Ann Tomlinson suggests that after we have begun our planning by looking at normative assessment results in conjunction with individual student performance, we use tiering activities when

---

2   Adapted from National Governors Association Center for Best Practices, *Common Core State Standards* (Washington, DC: Council of Chief State School Officers, 2010).

working with the same ideas and skills to ensure "all students focus on essential understandings and skills but at different levels of complexity, abstractness, and open-endedness."[3] Later, when we begin to identify assessment methods and plan for learning (steps two and three of Wiggins and McTighe's backward design method), teachers can then tailor instruction by tiering lessons with sound, differentiated teaching practices that will help guide all learners toward mastery.

Planning high allows every educator to easily answer yes to the question "Once differentiated, will this learning segment meet the needs of every student, *including* my highest?"

DESIGNING ANTIRACIST ASSESSMENTS AND LEARNING ACTIVITIES

The design of antiracist learning activities and assessments can be developed in the same way we design traditional content-area learning. While we are seeking to engage students in discoveries surrounding the impacts of individual and systemic racism on others, as educators, we must still seek to ensure learning has occurred by answering these questions:

- What is it that we want students to be able to show us that they understand?
- What skill are we inviting students to develop in order to show mastery?

The antiracist assessments and activities we design for students can be both formative and summative in nature. We want students to be able to participate in activities that help shape learning so that they feel confident when the time for evaluation of mastery arrives.

---

3   Carol A. Tomlinson, *The Differentiated Classroom: Responding to the Needs of All Learners* (Alexandria, VA: Association for Supervision and Curriculum Development, 1999), 83.

There are countless methods for bringing students clarity when answering the big questions surrounding racism, so it is important to consider how you will include these kinds of assessments alongside other classroom learning experiences. Will they be embedded in an existing learning segment? Or will you conduct a standalone assessment that allows students to show mastery around antiracism? There are many methods you might apply as you seek to bring about awareness through your content area:

- **Conversations, discussions, or Socratic seminars** surrounding concepts and topics related to antiracism in your content area are essential to helping students deepen their understanding.
- **Collaboration during project-based learning** can help students to develop tolerance and empathy, which supports the development of antiracist views.
- **Student research** of antiracist topics that are of interest to them can be easily included in content-area learning and can serve to broaden students' views and perspectives.
- **Performance-based assessments**—such as designing public service announcements (digital or print), conducting interviews, or writing and delivering scripted presentations (such as role playing or dramatic interpretation of historical events)—allow students to engage in authentic learning that will bring about lasting change.
- **Portfolios** can help students to observe their growth over time as it pertains to the development of their own antiracist attitudes and behaviors.

There's no limit to the amount of activities and assessments that support antiracist learning. Taking students on field trips, inviting guests into your learning space, and including literature, film, and music in your content-area teaching all enhance awareness of racism.

This learning also needs to be student centered in nature, too. Even when it comes to antiracism, give students choices regarding how they will learn and demonstrate mastery. They need a platform for sharing, in their own voices, what they have learned about antiracism, and they need to know that we have tailored this learning with their interests in mind. When we plan antiracist learning experiences in this way, we are doing more than bringing about awareness; we are creating change agents, truth-revealers, and advocates willing to stand up for what is right.

PLANNING POINTS TO REMEMBER

- **Take your time.** Weaving elements of antiracism and diversity into your content is a deliberate process. If you have not done this before, you may be reevaluating many of your lesson plans, new and old, through an entirely different lens.
- **Look for just one spot** in every lesson where you can allow students access to perspectives different from their own, where they will learn something about another race, ethnicity, or culture within the content.
- **You are not expected to have all the answers.** Remember, one of the best ways to learn is to do, so don't shy away from content that you are unfamiliar with yourself. This will be a process of growth for you, too.
- **You don't have to do it alone.** There are plenty of folks who are already on this journey or who are willing to go on it with you. They don't have to be in your building or even in your town. You simply need find them and invite them to join you. While this takes courage, just know there *is* someone out there waiting for your invitation.
- **Remember, students are experiencing their own transformational journey as well.** This will be tough for some students. Allow them time and space to process. Our task is to help build students up, not tear them down. In many cases, they'll be bringing many negative cultural constructs with them that they had no idea were wrong. We need to be delicate with them.

PLANNING DEEP

Once we have utilized student data to determine the varied levels of learners and have established the *why* behind our teaching, we must next consider the complexity of the activities in which we are asking students to engage. Yes, learning targets must be data-driven, but our learning targets must also provide the opportunity for students to complete tasks that push their levels of thinking, too. We can accomplish this by incorporating various levels of rigor and critical thinking into our teaching, pairing Webb's Depth of Knowledge framework and Bloom's Taxonomy to develop mastery targets for every learner. This is planning deep.

Webb's Depth of Knowledge

Webb's Depth of Knowledge (DOK) model provides a necessary methodology for scaffolding tasks and learning segments as a spiraling curriculum steeped in the advancement of critical thinking skills. It begins with simple tasks involving recollection and reproduction and continues through extensive critical thinking tasks that eventually require students to transform the knowledge they have acquired into something entirely new. In the simplest terms, DOK provides teachers with a framework for analyzing how much critical thinking a particular lesson, activity, or goal will require of students. DOK asks teachers to pay attention to the level of analysis involved in any goal or activity to ensure they are setting forth rigorous standards for learning in their classroom.

Erik Francis encourages educators to maintain a focus on context when using Webb's model to develop learning goals for their students. He provides educators with clarity on how to use DOK questioning to construct learning objectives that involve higher-order thinking and are tied directly to instructional content and standards. These questions are vital when framing student learning objectives so that educators are sure to have the right level of rigor within the context of the content for each DOK level. Francis divides the instructional focus of DOK levels into four distinct categories:

- DOK 1: What is the knowledge?
- DOK 2: How can the knowledge be used?
- DOK 3: How and why could the knowledge be used?
- DOK 4: How else could you use the knowledge?[4]

By considering these four questions as you plan, you can establish rigor even at the lowest level of learning, and when properly utilized, DOK targets become meaty and challenging, consisting of far more than a few simple verb-based stems. Deeper teaching and learning experiences will engage students to demonstrate higher levels of thinking up to and beyond the ceiling of assessment.

Bloom's Taxonomy

Webb's DOK is just one of the fundamentals for establishing rigor in your learning targets. Although it allows students to develop the kind of thinking that will transform understanding, Webb's framework on its own is not enough to generate learning targets that will engage students in positive, productive struggles.

Including Bloom's Taxonomy classifications of learning as we seek to identify outcomes and objectives as well as design assessments means that our learning goals will be measurable. Bloom's Taxonomy is the primary learning-targets tool we can use to measure students' knowledge, skills, and sometimes even their attitudes. Using Bloom's language in our objectives means we have invited students to do something that will give them the ability to demonstrate mastery of academic concepts and skills or to engage in learning that has been designed with the appropriate domain in mind.

---

4   Erik M. Francis, "Depth of Knowledge or Extent of Learning," Maverik Education blog, 2018, https://maverikeducation.com/blog/f/depth-of-knowledge-or-extent-of -learning.

Bloom's + Webb's = Mastery

Webb's DOK, with rigor at its core, and Bloom's Taxonomy, which uses verbs that serve to classify learning at different levels, make perfect partners when developing learning targets. Educators can use Bloom's verbs to guide what happens at each level of learning and DOK as a method to encourage deeper thinking during that learning. Simply put, Bloom's Taxonomy might cover the *doing* portion of the learning objective, while DOK covers the *thinking* portion of the objective. Using the below template as a guide, educators can create tailored learning objectives by filling in the target statements with content-specific *doing/thinking/mastery* combinations. For example, in an English 10 Greek Mythology unit, a mastery target might sound something like this:

> Students will be able to **analyze** (Bloom's) stories in Greek mythology in which they **synthesize ideas and interpret themes** (DOK) by **constructing an evidence-based, informative essay** (mastery) that explains how Greek mythology helped ancient people answer the questions that mystified them.

So then what does it look like when we put Bloom's and Webb's together to develop tiered learning targets? Remember those social studies benchmark results we looked at previously? Now that we understand how to develop solid learning targets, we can utilize those data-driven focal points to design learning targets for the highest tier of learners all the way down to the lowest, as in this example (adapted from a handbook from the Ohio Association for Gifted Children):

Tier 3 Learning Target

Students will reference multiple sources, including the internet, to **analyze** connections between the cultures of Britain, Japan, and Egypt until 1490 AD and **evaluate** how they might have influenced each other by **organizing and**

presenting a debate surrounding an issue relevant to the time period.

Tier 2 Learning Target

Students will examine at least two different resources to **identify and explain** the structures of the systems of government in Britain, Japan, and Egypt until 1490 AD and **interpret** how each type of government affected society by **creating a visual display** that represents each government's effect on its society.

Tier 1 Learning Target

Students will use an encyclopedia to **identify** five artists from Britain, Japan, and Egypt until 1490 AD and will **summarize** the contributions of each by **constructing one-page biographies and visual displays** that represents each artist's life story.[5]

We can see that tier three's learning target will meet the needs of our most advanced learners. From there, the remaining targets have been modified to meet the needs of learners who fell into the tiers two and one based on their assessment results.

While tailoring learning targets can involve in-depth analysis of data, it doesn't always have to. You also do not have to plan learning targets in this manner for every single lesson. However, when planning mastery-level summative assessments, this process is best. Tackling learning targets in this way ensures all learners' needs will be met, and the result is data-driven, authentic growth.

---

5   Adapted from Ohio Association for Gifted Children, *What to Expect When . . . You're Teaching a Gifted Child: A Handbook for Teachers of Gifted Children,* OAGC, 2013, oagc. com/wp-content/uploads/2021/07/WHAT-TO-EXPECT...Teacher-Handbook-8.24.2018.pdf.

CREATING ANTIRACIST LEARNING TARGETS

In the same way we plan for any other type of classroom learning, antiracist learning design should, without a doubt, include the use of targets to help you define your focus for mastery. This requires outside-the-standards-box thinking. In antiracist learning design, rather than looking at a set of standards from which you would extract learning targets within the context of your content, you may instead be sending students on a quest to understand some concept or big idea or to master a skill related to bringing them closer to an awareness of the effects of individual or systemic racism *through* your content.

Integrating threads of antiracism into your content is a deliberate act, and your goal is for students to come away with a heightened sense of awareness surrounding race or racism. However, when we aim to assess understanding, we can face challenges due to the sometimes ambiguous nature and moving definition of exactly what *understanding* can mean. There may be a right or wrong to understanding, but when we seek to assess based on one's perceptions, the way we handle misunderstandings or misinterpretations can lead to an inability to effectively evaluate or provide students with helpful feedback. That said, when assessing for understanding, your learning targets should be crystal clear through the use of concise expectations and zero obscurity in mastery language.

In conjunction with understanding, antiracism education also allows for skills development, a process that is somewhat easier to assess for mastery. For example, through their study of antiracism, equity, or social injustice, students might learn to

- Distinguish between types of racism: individual acts versus structural
- Identify racism and microaggressions

- Define culture and evaluate historical perspectives[6]

This should not prevent you from designing learning around understanding, though. A focus on understanding has the potential to impact students on a deeply personal level, and this is exactly what we should be shooting for. The same learning-target methodology still applies, however, you may or may not have tiered targets for these learning segments. For example:

> From **analyzing** (Bloom's) informational texts, students will be able to **distinguish between** (Webb's) structural racism and individual racist actions by **creating an infographic** that **outlines** the characteristics of each (mastery).

PLANNING WIDE

So far in this process, we have analyzed student data to identify learner categories and grouped students to establish developmentally appropriate learning targets. Those targets have been reverse-engineered, tiered, and crafted with rigor in mind using Webb's DOK and Bloom's Taxonomy. Our final goal in designing learning should be to provide the kinds of student-centered learning opportunities that will not only meet learners where they are but also allow them to show their full potential. Developing a wide array of formative and summative assessments that guide students toward mastery is important, for sure, but we can't stop there. The assessments we design for students must promote inclusivity as well as take into consideration what is important to students as individuals. Most importantly, we must design those assessments and learning activities with students as the focal point.

---

6 Lewis-Clark State College, "Teaching Antiracism," Center for Teaching and Learning, lcsc. edu/teaching-learning/inclusion-diversity-equity-antiracism/teaching-antiracism.

A Student-Centered Approach to Inclusivity

We have many different types of learners within our classrooms, some of whom come to us with labels already attached to them. Some students arrive to us with disabilities that entitle them to a support system that might involve individualized education plans, 504 plans, or some other accommodation framework. Others may be labeled as gifted or English-as-a-second-language learners. Learners come from diverse backgrounds, which may include a broad range of values, traditions, and belief systems that fall outside those of the dominant culture. That said, our students rely on us to provide them with a wide array of learning experiences that will aid them in reaching their individual learning goals. But regardless of labels, we must remember that these students are people first, and our ability to create a learning environment that makes each one of them feel as if they belong is mission critical.

When we provide authentic, student-centered activities, students may be more inclined to invest their time and energy into whatever task we encourage them to undertake. You have worked hard to provide them with outstanding data-driven, tailored targets, so you'll want to make sure students are willing to partake in whatever learning you have designed. If you do, their time, and yours, will be well spent.

Student-centered learning should involve inquiry, reflection, and celebrating our differences in the context of classroom learning, but we also need to be willing to go further. Engaging students in collaboration, supporting their individual learning styles, and allowing them to share their stories are a few ways in which we can help students feel as if they are part of a learning environment that values them in every way.

STUDENTS ARE PEOPLE FIRST

Use Collaboration to Foster Belonging

Create a culture of belonging by making collaboration common during learning. When students collaborate, they not only develop important skills that support their success in the classroom, like active listening and oral communication, but more importantly, they build stronger relationships with their peers, which strengthens the overall culture and sense of belonging in your classroom.

Support Individual Learning Styles

Help students tap into their individual learning styles as they complete activities and assessments. Allow your visual learners to submit images, drawings, or artwork that demonstrates their progress toward goals. Allow those with linguistic strengths to record audio submissions in which they provide oral examples of mastery.

Weaving various types of learning profiles into the activities you design allows you not only to reach every student but also to offer them practice with other learning styles. Talk with students about the different ways in which they learn, and discuss the value that each of their styles brings to the classroom and to the work they will do in the future. Also invite them to discuss how their passions are influenced by how they feel they best learn.

Promote the Sharing of Stories

To promote inclusivity, allow students the space to share their stories within the context of your content. Stories about our lives can tie to any subject we teach at school. Include the telling of those stories within the formative assessments. Invite students to share how math or science comes into play while they are engaged in a hobby or sport. Ask how English or social studies helped them to have a stronger, more informed discussion with someone. Show them, through their own stories, the value of the content that you bring to them.

Let Students Tell You How They Need to Learn

Each year I provide students with a survey that asks them a number of questions about themselves as learners. Their responses usually give me an indication of the kinds of assessments students enjoy, how they like to engage with learning, and how they perceive their education overall—that is, what matters and what doesn't. When we ask students what is important to them before we design learning experiences, we can tailor learning in a way that shows we are responding to students' needs and interests. Some of the questions I like to ask students are

- What do you feel is the most important part of your education? Where do you feel your teachers should focus their attention as it pertains to your own personal education?
- What type of learner would you say you are? Are you better with hands-on kinds of activities? Do visuals or audio help you? Do you work better with others or on your own?
- What do you enjoy most about school? What do you enjoy least about school?
- What kinds of learning activities engage you the most? In other words, what makes learning fun and motivates you to want to learn?
- What do you wish people knew about you as a learner?

With the answers to these kinds of questions, you have the ability to discern what activities will work best for specific learner groups. Using the learning targets you identified for each learner group and information from surveys like this, you can adjust group assessments to reflect the needs of each group's learners. Knowing what engages and motivates students can also be helpful when preparing student-selected assessments, as this information can be used when designing assessment options. When students recognize that you have taken their interests and needs into consideration in your learning and assessment design, engagement *and* growth will simultaneously improve.

PLAN HIGH, DEEP, AND WIDE FOR ANTIRACIST LEARNING, TOO

Every single content area can offer opportunities to explore matters of racism, inequity, social injustice, racial disparities, and social issues that impact marginalized populations, and this shouldn't be omitted from our day-to-day planning. The process of integrating antiracist threads into your teaching is much the same as designing other learning experiences for your students, and the steps outlined throughout this chapter are applicable to antiracist teaching and learning, too.

As you consider the *what*, *why*, and *how* of antiracist learning within your curriculum, remember that your primary objective is to invite students to examine the effects of individual and structural/systemic racism on the conditions and circumstances of others. We can do this in every content area:

Math: What kinds of statistics or mathematical data can you analyze with regard to racism? Think about how word problems you present or stories you read and analyze in math class paint a picture of systemic racism and social injustices that keep certain groups marginalized or oppressed. Then engage students in the coordinating math lessons.

Science: What scientific topics can you present that highlight the impact of science on systemic racism? Which Black and ethnic minority scientists can you introduce students to? Find articles that connect the various forms of racism to the science curriculum. These things are often only a Google search away.

Social studies: This subject area may make the most sense when we think about introducing students to issues surrounding equity, antiracism, and social justice. The opportunities are abundant, mostly because antiracism directly correlates with history *and* people. What silenced voices can you allow students to finally hear? What stories can you share that offer alternative perspectives? Where in the curriculum can you allow students to see how historically marginalized people have been intentionally left out of the shaping of the dominant culture?

Health and physical education: What are some of the major health issues that affect minority populations? How are our perceptions of the physical ability and health and wellness of others shaped by our biases? What impact does lack of access to healthy food choices (i.e., food deserts) have on communities of color? Why do these exist in the first place?

English: This subject offers an amazing opportunity to explore the lives of others through literature, informational texts, and even some visual media. We need not look any further than the words of Rudine Sims Bishop, who helps us see the power of literature in the development of tolerance and empathy:

> Books are sometimes windows, offering views of worlds that may be real or imagined, familiar or strange. These windows are also sliding glass doors, and readers have only to walk through in imagination to become part of whatever world has been created or re-created by the author. When lighting conditions are just right, however, a window can also be a mirror. Literature transforms human experience and reflects it back to us, and in that reflection we can see our own lives and experiences as part of a larger human experience. Reading, then, becomes a means of self-affirmation, and readers often seek their mirrors in books.[7]

The process of designing a well-rounded antiracist curriculum begins with you taking deliberate steps to educate yourself with regard to the facts surrounding racism, discrimination, and other topics like privilege, racial and social injustice, and inequality, so that you can be more informed as you seek to include antiracism into your content.

---

7 Rudine Sims Bishop, quoted in Violet J. Harris, "In Praise of a Scholarly Force: Rudine Sims Bishop," *Language Arts* 85, no. 2 (November 2007): 153–59, https://library.ncte.org/journals/LA/issues/v85-2/6175.

However, you can't wait to begin until you feel like you have completed your education in this area, for two reasons: First, you won't. Second, kids can't afford for you to wait. You can learn right alongside them. When planning for learning, if you want to embed antiracism into a learning segment but you are struggling with where to find support in doing so, try something as simple as Googling key phrases, such as:

- Systemic racism shaped by {subject}
- Antiracism education in {subject} class

There are countless resources and organizations to help you with this process just a click away on the internet. Seek help from others who are already doing this work, or check in with allies to work through your planning together. Visit the Antiracism Education Resource Library at www.educationundone.com for helpful links to support you as you work to integrate antiracist teaching and learning into your curriculum.

DIFFERENTIATING WITH FIDELITY

The number of ways in which we can differentiate assessment and classroom learning are endless. Each day we can employ new methods of supporting students through learning experiences we have tailored to their individual needs, such as varied content delivery methods, unique products, adjusted timelines, gamification, and learning stations, just to name a few. What is especially important is that we are consistent in our application of differentiation so that we can observe student growth. Through our consistency, we should be able to clearly see this growth based on the unique learning opportunities we have designed for our students. And while we may not be differentiating learning targets on an everyday basis, the ways in which we approach teaching and learning *should* be differentiated daily. Students should come to expect that every learning experience we provide has been designed with their needs in mind. Differentiating with fidelity and consistency are necessary commitments that will have a lasting impact on learning.

DROP ANCHOR

Think about an upcoming learning segment you plan to introduce to students.

- ⚒ What information does preassessment data reveal to you about your learners with regard to content you are considering introducing?
- ⚒ What does the data say students are struggling to do, and how will you use this to create your learning targets? How will you need to adjust your focus within each tier of learners based on what the data says?
- ⚒ What concepts or skills will this lesson help students develop?
- ⚒ What has the potential to be a good example of an inclusive, student-centered assessment that will allow all learners to show mastery of the target you have designed?
- ⚒ How can you connect this learning with matters related to diversity, race and racism, or differing cultural perspectives? Where in *your* content can you
    - ⚒ Allow students the opportunity to learn about someone different from themselves?
    - ⚒ Present and compare facts, ideas, or perspectives from different types of individuals or cultures?
    - ⚒ Expose students to cultural norms that are different from their own?
- ⚒ What type of summative assessments and/or formative learning activities can you design to ensure understanding of the antiracist concepts or skills you present to students?

PART III

Do It

IMPLEMENT WITH
PRECISION

FIVE

Navigate Learning with the Essential Eight

*The greatest sign of success for a teacher . . .
is to be able to say, "The children are
now working as if I did not exist."*
—MARIA MONTESSORI

*F*ocusing on a strong design for learning involves making use of the most effective practices possible to help every student successfully navigate learning in our classroom. This means utilizing a practical framework that ensures that no matter what we ask students to learn, they are successful in doing so because the stops we have planned for them on their journey leave them with applicable knowledge and skills that will last them a lifetime.

PIRATE planners know how to design tailored learning experiences that present students with relevant content and concepts that will transform how they think and how they view the world around them. As a PIRATE planner, the learning you design will have value in the eyes of your students because you will have engaged them in thinking about the importance of that learning and, when all is said and done, they will leave your space with unforgettable experiences that will provide them support for the rest of their lives. PIRATE planning means we have not just taken deliberate steps to prepare engaging and informative learning experiences for our students, but we will also be there to guide them in that learning all along the way.

THE EIGHT ESSENTIAL PRACTICES OF GREAT TEACHING

I remember, years ago, my very first teaching job was in a small, open-enrollment district that served primarily Black and Brown students from the outskirts of Dayton, Ohio. It was far from cutting-edge. It was underfunded, under-resourced, and for sure under-air-conditioned! None of this got in the way of my excitement, however. I spent late summer that year working in my sweltering classroom as I prepared for the ninth-, eleventh-, and twelfth-grade students who would enter it that August. One humid afternoon, as I struggled to get some freshly laminated posters to stick to the cinderblock walls, Mr. G, our administrator, came in to check on me. He looked around a bit, complimented my room, and before leaving, said, "I know this is your first year in the classroom, and I have tremendous faith in you. You're going to do great, but I want to give you something that may help you this year." He handed me a list with a number of teaching practices printed on it that he said were shown to improve student growth and achievement. This list turned out to be very beneficial to my own growth as a first-year teacher as well. Some of the practices I used, others not at all. But over time, as I have worked to improve my teaching, the list has morphed into my own framework of nonnegotiable practices that I embed into my teaching every single day. I refer to them as the Essential Eight:

1. Facilitate concept-based learning.
2. Encourage critical thinking and inquiry.
3. Infuse academic and content vocabulary.
4. Integrate technology purposefully.
5. Connect learning with constructed responses.

6. Provide meaningful, high-quality feedback.
7. Build strong relationships.
8. Establish a bell-to-bell learning environment.

The Essential Eight framework is not meant to supplant well-designed lesson plans, but rather is an assortment of practices to commit to daily that will help you guide students through the learning you have planned so that it sticks. The core components of education that we have worked so hard to master—many of which we've talked about in previous chapters, such as differentiation and well-designed, developmentally appropriate assessments—will always be an inherent part of our planning. The Essential Eight framework simply makes certain that all the learning you planned and intend to execute gets through to every student.

The depth of learning that takes place when these eight practices are used together is undeniable. They can be easily integrated into your existing lesson plans and are designed to work within any content area. So, whether you are teaching students how physics applies to daily life or how they can skillfully manage their money for a more financially secure future, this engaging framework will allow students to take control of and easily navigate their own learning.

ESSENTIAL PRACTICE #1: FACILITATE CONCEPT-BASED LEARNING

To help students become stronger, more creative, solution-oriented critical thinkers, we must present them with real-world learning through concept-based teaching of relevant ideas. When we offer students the opportunity to explore ideas on their own, within the context of the content we teach, we are allowing them to construct their own meaning as opposed to pushing our ideas or understanding on them. Giving students the freedom to make meaning through their own investigation and interpretation of information makes learning truly student centered. This process creates students who are excited about learning because they are the ones in control of it. Our role is to help them tie that learning to other disciplines and their own personal interests so that they are able to use it to make meaning of the world that surrounds them.

Strategies for Implementation

Set up units by themes.

In units like the Psychology of Fear, students investigate the science behind being scared and how it connects to the thrills we feel when reading horror stories or watching films of the horror genre. In this unit, not only do students engage in reading informational texts and a number of stories from the genre, but they also evaluate varying types of fear that take hold of their minds and discover how fear affects them physically, emotionally, and psychologically. After assessing horror story writings of others, students write their own horror narratives incorporating specific categories of fear. This unit is fully standards based, incorporating many elements of English language arts study; completely concept based, e.g., fear can hold tremendous power over individuals; and wholly student centered as students get to explore fear in the context of their own lives.

Design projects that center on big ideas.

Invite students into broad learning experiences through projects like the School of Tomorrow, where they engage in research related to the school experience in the United States compared with that of other places in the world. This project can serve as cross-curricular with other content areas such as math, where students use geometry principles to design buildings, or social sciences like psychology, where students include their understanding of the social-emotional effect schooling has on children. Have students practice their written communication skills by preparing letters to school leaders in which they voice their opinions about how their school should change to meet the needs of its learners.

Create connections by comparing experiences.
This can involve asking students at any point to compare and contrast their own experiences using your curriculum as the lens through which they examine them. Why does this matter? Because when we do this, students begin to realize they are more alike than different. Kids may be less fearful of engaging in collaborative learning when they know more about one another and when they know they share things in common. In English class, host a poetry contest where students create and perform two-voice poems that highlight each of their views, their cultures, or their beliefs, side by side. In social studies class, spend time discussing students' perceptions of periods in history or their take on current events in anticipation of new learning segments. Comparing experiences and perspectives helps build the kind of empathy necessary to create a strong antiracist classroom culture, too.

By generating learning segments that focus on concepts and big ideas, we take the focus of instruction off the skill and allow students to engage in learning in the context of important topics within our content and to join these with ideas that are intriguing to them. When we employ this practice, students become more connected to the learning and to each other as they explore ideas through a multitude of perspectives.

Reflect on Your Practice

- What are some existing skills-based units of study you have created that might easily be converted to concept-based units?
- How can you engage students in the process of designing their own concept-based learning segments? What input can they contribute that will help you shape learning experiences for them?
- Concept-based teaching and learning requires additional planning time up front to make connections between your content and the big ideas you wish to share with students. How might

you begin planning these experiences without feeling like you have to overhaul your entire curriculum?

- With whom in your department or your building might you build out cross-curricular, concept-based units of learning? Which departments make the most sense to partner with based on the content and big ideas you wish to share?

ESSENTIAL PRACTICE #2: ENCOURAGE CRITICAL THINKING AND INQUIRY

When we ask students to think critically in the classroom, we are asking them to examine questions and problems inside and out in order to find solutions in order to gain lasting understanding of our content. Critical thinking allows individuals to engage in meaningful discussion and to interpret complex ideas. Putting critical thinking into action in the classroom means students get to practice analyzing questions by constructing clear answers; they get to dig deeper than the background knowledge they possess when providing those answers; and they can make judgments about the credibility of the sources and inputs they examine. Our goal should be to help students learn to communicate and defend their perspectives by the close of critical inquiry.

Asking kids to think critically comes with the need for rigorous and engaging questions; however, we must be sure those questions tie students' thinking directly to the content presented. In this case, guiding questions relate directly to key ideas within the content area or discipline and foster critical thinking about the subject or topic. Guiding questions can, and should, be student centered, allowing students to contribute individual experiences and background knowledge when they are asked to provide input. These overarching questions should be interesting enough to compel students to want to go deeper into their search for meaning or understanding in the context of learning. Guiding questions can serve as the backbone of any lesson or unit and should most definitely serve to spark students' curiosity.

Strategies for Implementation

Start with why.

Ask students to create a *why* question they would like to know the answer to or that they think they might enjoy researching. Students will come up with some great examples like "If school is supposed to be a place where students enjoy coming every day, why isn't it enjoyable for some students?" or "Why do some people choose to hate?" These questions can be fantastic launch points for problem-based or service-learning projects.

Pose thick rather than thin questions.

As often as possible, avoid giving students closed-ended questions. Try to skip the what, where, and when questions and replace them with stems like *what if, how might*, or *why do you think*. How and why questions are obviously better questions for challenging students' thinking about the topics we present to them, especially when we ask them to provide supporting details or evidence. Turn question exploration into a competition. Ask students to take sides. Put them on opposite sides of your room based on their choices, and name the team with the best reasons and supporting evidence the "Defending" Champions.

Model your own critical thinking.

When teaching kids to think critically, it is imperative that we demonstrate for them what that process looks like. Try walking students through your own thought process when sorting through issues or ideas. Allow them to hear how you came to a conclusion by using phrases like "This was confusing, but now I understand that . . ." Invite students into your thought process and ask them for help as you solve problems aloud.

Host Socratic seminars.

This group discussion strategy allows students to vocalize their critical thinking collectively. Give students time to prepare responses ahead of the discussion, and then arrange them in either large or small groups where they can share their findings and bounce ideas off one another. Socratic seminars can be done at any grade level and in any content area.

Steer thinking with guiding questions.

Guiding questions are imperative for connecting students with the content you share with them, acting as a compass that helps them to navigate learning in the classroom. By providing these rigorous, content-based questions, we give students the opportunity to broaden their understanding by using their background knowledge combined with the new findings they discover. When we invite students to engage with guiding questions, we are preparing them to be conscientious and curious thinkers with a desire to make meaning from our content and to find answers to their questions as well.

Utilize graphic organizers.

When providing students with essential questions surrounding a lesson or a unit's content, it is important that we provide them space to categorize information and ideas. Graphic organizers allow students to arrange their thoughts around essential questions, especially when we ask them to brainstorm, compare/contrast, or sequence. Graphic organizers such as Venn diagrams, T-charts, outline templates, cause-and-effect charts, and bubble diagrams can provide students structure for their discussions and writing about critical questions.

Just like adults, kids are also faced with making minute-by-minute decisions based on the media they see, hear, and interact with daily. In this digital era, students are continually bombarded by information from a multitude of sources: news, radio, television, social media, magazines, and more. By teaching students to become conscientious critical thinkers, we are helping them to develop the skills they need to navigate a complicated and sometimes deceptive world. As critical thinkers, they will be able to come to logical conclusions and develop an enhanced understanding of the world around them. Ultimately, by teaching them to think critically, our students will become empathetic, insightful, and aware.

Reflect on Your Practice

- What methods do you use to determine the questions you choose for students, and how do you incorporate higher-order thinking into your content-area question structure?
- How have you been proactive in helping students improve their critical thinking skills?
- Think about an upcoming lesson you have planned for students. What techniques can you incorporate to help foster critical thinking in the learning segment?
- Think back to your last lesson or unit. What were some of the guiding questions you posed to students? Were they thick questions or thin ones?
- Revisiting those questions, how could you revise the language to make them more rigorous in the context of the curriculum?

ESSENTIAL PRACTICE #3: INFUSE ACADEMIC AND CONTENT VOCABULARY

If we help students to grasp the meaning of the language, we also build their confidence in their ability to express what they know. When students recognize and understand academic language, they will be able to better prepare for and complete assessments because they can identify what is being asked of them. When they understand the language involved in the exploration of content, they will be more willing to engage with other learners because they can successfully articulate their thoughts. Building time into the curriculum for students to explore both academic and domain-specific language means they will be able to construct responses that reflect their growth and show their mastery of concepts and skills.

Regular use of academic language improves students' understanding of how to interact with questions and content in the context of learning. Academic language is more than just test language. It involves a working knowledge of word relationships, root words, words with multiple meanings, connotative/denotative meanings, and figurative language. In addition, students need to be able to dissect more abstract language that asks them to engage deeply with the curriculum. Task words such as *analyze, infer, judge, evaluate, classify, compare,* etc. should be part of students' daily language in the classroom, as this vocabulary will allow students to tap into their potential and improve their overall growth.

Domain-specific or content-related vocabulary is language specific to the subject or discipline you teach. In English class, these might be words such as *onomatopoeia, theme,* or *dramatic irony.* In math, these could be words like *rational numbers, functions,* or *inequalities.* While you won't have to look far for domain-specific vocabulary (just open any textbook), you do need to make sure that the words you choose for students are necessary to their understanding of what they will learn. Choosing the right domain-specific words means you have determined learning targets prior to lesson plan development and the language you have selected ties directly to those targets. Students should see and hear the words you choose for them during instruction, and by the end of learning, they should have a grasp of their importance for understanding the content.

Strategies for Implementation

Create an academic word wall.

Carve out a space in your classroom where you can put a list of the academic words you'll be using all year long. Introduce these words early in the year and leave them up for reference. Include them in your classroom activities, tasks, and daily communication with students. Administer an academic language diagnostic assessment early on to determine where and how much instructional focus is necessary.

Use academic language everywhere.

Be deliberate in the discussion and instruction of academic language. When talking with students, use the language you wish for them to become familiar with in the classroom. Start by replacing common language with academic synonyms. For example, instead of *arrange*, you might use the word *classify*; instead of *speak*, try *communicate*—in context, of course. When appropriate, be dramatic or silly to make it stick.

Break apart questions.

Invite students to identify what is being asked of them and the proper ways to respond. Ask them to investigate not only what the academic language means but what would be required of them in order to provide an adequate response.

Read rigorous texts.

Providing students with nonfiction texts related to the content area will expose them to plenty of academic and domain-specific vocabulary. There are a wide range of resources for nonfiction texts, including websites like CommonLit.org or Newsela.com, online journals and newspapers as well as online encyclopedias.

Integrate vocabulary into questions.

Be thoughtful and deliberate in how you construct questions so they serve to advance learning. Make sure you incorporate both academic and domain-specific language as you generate thought-provoking, rigorous questions. Throughout learning, be sure to give students ample opportunities to figure out word meanings using both connotation and denotation. When posing questions that use content-related vocabulary, offer students resources and research time so they are confident in providing responses that demonstrate they understand the vocabulary.

Students who have a command of academic and domain-specific language are more capable of dissecting complex questions and tasks. While informal communication has an important place in the classroom and should not be eliminated from daily discourse, using formal language allows students to connect with one another within the context of the curriculum and to bond through the sharing of ideas. A strong vocabulary sets students up for success beyond the classroom, into college, and throughout their careers. Having a command of language means students have the ability to communicate across disciplines to share what they understand about the complexities of the world around them.

If we do not take the time to help students understand the language of our content and the academic language necessary to demonstrate mastery of new knowledge and skills, we risk losing students entirely. We cannot expect students to grow when we are attempting to engage them by using language they do not understand.

Reflecting on Your Practice

- In what ways do you engage students in the acquisition and understanding of vocabulary in the context of your classroom learning activities?
- What academic language have you already introduced students to so far this year? How would you rate your students' overall proficiency in terms of their knowledge of academic language? How do you know this?
- What strategies could you use to help improve students' command of academic language at this point in the school year?
- How do you incorporate domain-specific vocabulary into your teaching at present? What would you say is the impact of this practice? How has this helped your students with learning?
- If teaching domain-specific vocabulary is not part of your practice, how might you approach building this into your instruction?

ESSENTIAL PRACTICE #4: INTEGRATE TECHNOLOGY PURPOSEFULLY

As we learned in chapter three, technology in the classroom can be used for so many things: a vehicle for the dissemination of information, a tool for helping students turn learning into creations, and even a way to keep students organized so they are able to remain fully engaged in learning at all times. Regardless of how we invite students to interact with technology, we must remember that technology itself should never be a solo act. Technology's job is to provide the kind of support that enhances the learning experience.

The technology we choose for students shouldn't distract them from learning, nor should it remove the much-needed social aspect of learning in the classroom. Students should also have a clear understanding of why you have chosen a particular tech tool to facilitate learning, and the technology you choose should allow students to engage with learning in ways that inspire them and help them acquire new knowledge and develop new skills. Technology has the power to provide unique avenues for the delivery of instruction that meets the needs of a variety of learner types; however, educators must be sure that the choice of technology used within a learning segment serves to advance learning as a whole. When choosing technology to support instruction, educators should have a clearly defined reason for doing so. Consider asking yourself, "If I were to facilitate this learning segment minus this technology, would outcomes be the same or different, and what impact will this form of technology have on my students' learning?"

Strategies for Implementation

Create real-world projects with tech.

Have kids use technology to create things they might make if they were at work in the real world. For instance, they could make websites that include content-specific information, create public service announcements, or develop informative/entertaining videos, podcasts, or even video games that focus on current classroom topics.

Assess with technology.

Incorporate assessment technology that allows you to gather important data that you can use to evaluate your students' skills as well as your effectiveness as their teacher. Websites like Edulastic.com, GoFormative.com, PlayPosit.com, and Flipgrid.com are just a few that allow you to assess students in both traditional and nontraditional ways. The options for integrating assessment technology into our instruction are endless, and new platforms emerge every day that easily allow educators to formatively and summatively assess learners in a variety of ways. Perform a quick Google search of "online assessment tools for education" and you'll be busy for hours discovering new methods for collecting student data!

Use digital media to enhance teaching and engage learners.

This can mean including videos to enhance interest when introducing students to new topics and skills or allowing students to create their own media to demonstrate the understanding they have developed through their classroom learning experiences.

Using technology in the right way can improve student engagement, provide educators with quick yet detailed feedback on student performance, and enhance student learning experiences while preparing them for their future careers. While an important part of twenty-first-century classrooms, technology must be implemented with fidelity and intentionality to ensure that it is fostering growth as opposed to simply "jazzing up" a learning segment.

Reflecting on Your Practice

- How do you utilize technology in your classroom now? Reflect on whether the ways in which you incorporate technology are purposeful and evaluate whether or not that enhances students' learning experiences.

- Think about a recent lesson in which you did not use technology. How might the learning segment have been improved if you had?

ESSENTIAL PRACTICE #5: CONNECT LEARNING WITH CONSTRUCTED RESPONSES

Regular practice composing constructed responses helps students gain confidence in their ability to articulate their thinking. When students are given time to structure their thoughts and are not forced to give on-demand answers, they will feel more comfortable engaging in discussion and sharing those thoughts. Students who have taken the time to put into writing answers to the questions we pose are not only practicing an important life skill but are also learning to sort out the noise inside their heads and pull out the most important details.

Constructed response questions should not be strictly reserved for essay-length writing assignments. Offer students the opportunity to create shorter evidence-based responses as well. Consider bell-ringers or exit slips in addition to full-length pieces of writing. Constructed responses serve as an extension of critical thinking by requiring students to articulate their thinking via their writing skills. Short constructed responses may consist of as few as three to five sentences, while extended constructed responses might require as many as five fully developed paragraphs that compose an evidence-based argument or detail-oriented informational text. Regardless of form or length, students need the opportunity each day to put their thoughts into words in order to engage in higher-order thinking while broadening their knowledge in the content area.

Strategies for Implementation

Answer autopsies.

In math class, have students analyze incorrect answers and put into words where the errors in their calculations occurred. Ask them to explain how they could correctly solve the problem using words instead of numeric problem-solving.

Anticipatory sets.

Before introducing a new learning segment, pose a brief but rigorous question related to the new content. Have students put their thoughts and background knowledge into writing. When it's time to share, have them use their written responses to guide their oral ones.

Craft interpretations.

Ask students to analyze what they see in charts, graphs, or other visual representations and to summarize their findings via a written response.

In order for students to become proficient at anything, they must practice it. This same thing is true when it comes to writing. When we ask students to write something every day, they have the opportunity to tap into their critical thinking skills and thereby internalize the information we present to them. Constructed responses require students to understand proper writing structure and to be able to analyze and evaluate what information they will need to formulate their answers—both important skills that will serve students throughout their lives.

By failing to ask our students to write every day, we are stripping them of the chance to learn how to transform their thoughts into words, which helps to improve their ability to be more succinct in sharing their thinking. If we want students to feel confident in what they do in our classrooms, we must give them the time and space necessary to formulate their own ideas and opinions, in writing, about the things we discuss with them in class. They need to write thoughts down if we truly want them to retain them.

KEY POINTS TO REMEMBER ABOUT CONSTRUCTED RESPONSES

❀ These don't have to be long writing assignments. Sometimes a few sentences are enough.

❀ Challenge students to always support their answers with evidence. Make sure even short argumentative responses have a clearly defined claim, followed by evidence to support the claim, and reasoning that further helps them prove that they are right.

❀ Make language and grammar the focus only when it is necessary. Are you asking students to demonstrate mastery of grammar or to show you what they understand? This is an important distinction when it comes to providing feedback.

Reflecting on Your Practice

- In your subject area, what are some ways in which you can build constructed responses into your curriculum so that students are able to use their writing to gain confidence when engaging in classroom discussions and learning?
- What types of constructed response opportunities do you provide students in your classroom daily? How do these allow students to communicate their thinking about concepts and classroom topics you present to them?
- How do you evaluate their mastery of those concepts based on the written responses they provide?

ESSENTIAL PRACTICE #6: PROVIDE MEANINGFUL, HIGH-QUALITY FEEDBACK

Meaningful, high-quality feedback can address whole-class, small-group, or individual progress toward learning objectives. It should motivate and encourage students, not deflate or demoralize them. When we provide students with meaningful feedback, they will perform better overall because they will know exactly where to focus when it comes to learning goals. Our feedback will help students to become more reflective and will improve both their motivation and engagement.

Strategies for Implementation

Conference individually and in small groups.
Build time into your schedule to provide face-to-face feedback. While this can be done individually, it's okay to break students into small groups for feedback, too.

Use quick-response feedback tools.
Try online or tech-based tools like Quizizz or Plickers to give assessments that provide instant, presentable data. Many of these tools offer the option to collect this data for later use. With online platforms such as these, both you and your students can gain immediate access to assessment results.

Create a data wall.
To keep everyone focused, post whole-group goals and share whole-class results. Remember to never post individual student data. Make the wall interactive so that monitoring progress is a live activity where students can see how the entire class is improving together. Celebrate your success when a classroom goal is met!

When students are able to see whole-class progress, they can evaluate their own growth compared to the whole. For teachers, sharing class data can help keep the focus on efficacy and growth in relationship to instructional practices and student learning. While students should also have access to individual tracking tools to gauge progress, teachers should be active in monitoring students' individual performance to identify at-risk students. The analysis of individual student data against learning targets can help teachers identify areas where reteaching or individualized instruction is needed. When done properly, sharing data is a great way to help motivate students to focus on growth and mastery.

Don't forget to provide students with support when they are falling short, and refrain from using phrases like "well done" or "good job." Instead, use feedback starters like:

"That's a great start, but perhaps you could try . . ."
"You're on the right track, but maybe take a look here for additional information . . ."

Or ask questions such as:

"Can you tell me about how you came to this conclusion?"
"Help me understand why you chose this answer?"

This kind of language helps students embrace mistakes while learning exactly where to focus attention to show progress toward goals. Helping students realize their successes in the form of timely and relevant feedback will create confidence and help them better understand how to refine their work. The quality of the feedback we provide is vital to student growth.

Reflecting on Your Practice

- How often do you share or discuss assessment data with your students?
- Right now, what data could you share with students that could serve to motivate them or enhance their focus on specific areas of learning?

- Thinking ahead to your next lesson, how might you plan to provide meaningful, high-quality feedback with students that will give them a clearer picture of their progress in your content area?

ESSENTIAL PRACTICE #7: BUILD STRONG RELATIONSHIPS

When we embed relationship building and classroom culture into all facets of learning, we create a safe and inviting environment for all students. Students who feel that the classroom is a safe space where their teacher knows them and has taken the time to design educational experiences specific to their needs and interests are willing to make an investment in learning. They will give us their all because they feel cared about and even loved.

One of the most significant factors involved in building positive relationships with students is our own authenticity. Kids can easily detect whether or not we are sincere in our approach to relationship building. We must be sure to come to students with a real desire to connect and to get to know them in ways that show we care. Students need to be able to trust us with their personal stories and struggles. This means we have to share our stories with them, too.

> STUDENTS NEED TO BE ABLE TO TRUST US WITH THEIR PERSONAL STORIES AND STRUGGLES. THIS MEANS WE HAVE TO SHARE OUR STORIES WITH THEM, TOO.

Strategies for Implementation

Explore HEARTS before Heads.

This fantastic activity by Lindsay Portnoy, author of *Designed to Learn*, asks students to share important details of their life with you so that you and students can learn more about one another. The wonderful thing about this process is that it has the potential to help build strong classroom connections. During the activity, students reveal information about their HEARTS—home, educational experiences, activities, reasons for learning, and transformative life experiences—which can be easily recorded using a simple graphic organizer. The premise of this activity is that before educators engage students in using their heads, it is helpful to know what is on their HEARTS, but at the same time, relationships evolve as a result of what students choose to share about their lives. I would add that this is a great activity for teachers to participate in, too. Students want to know about you as much as you want to know about them, so don't be afraid to share *your* HEARTS before Heads stories![1]

Utilize technology to support relationship building.

With the help of technology, it is easy to work on building strong and trusting student-student and student-teacher relationships. Try using tech-based learning platforms such as Pear Deck to create student interest inventories that will help you get to know more about your students. Allow students to collaborate digitally—presentations, websites, documents, etc.—when completing assessments so they can get to know each other better during collaboration, too. Share personalized notes via typed comments when providing assessment feedback in online platforms like Google Classroom. Allow students to participate in back-channel discussions using tools like Padlet throughout instructional segments so they can build relationships during their conversations about your content.

---

1   Lindsay Portnoy, "Three Tools for Learning during Uncertain Times," blog post, https://designed2learn.co/portblog/tag/hearts+before+heads, accessed October 11, 2021.

Don't shy away from tough conversations.

When students present us with difficult questions or delicate topics, they are telling us they care about something, so we can't ignore or dismiss them. Make sure to focus on the development of communication skills in your classroom early on. Teach students strategies for handling objections and opinions that differ from their own. When you allow tough conversations, students will value the time you give to help them reach an understanding of even the most difficult topics or issues. If you have done the work to create a culture of belonging in your classroom, one that is empathetic and that values diversity, tough conversations won't really be that tough and, in fact, can serve as transformational learning experiences for students and for you.

Create a Culture that Embraces Antiracism

Antiracist classrooms have many traits, but a few of them are imperative in helping us to carry out our mission. The following characteristics will ensure you have created a space where students are ready and able to embark on the journey to awareness and understanding:

Create a relationship-centered culture. Culture building begins with you. Ask yourself, *What opportunities am I creating that will allow me to get to know my students and my students to get to know one another?*

Teach students that discomfort is part of the process. Allowing students to engage in antiracist learning experiences can be uncomfortable, but we owe it to our students to bring them to an understanding of the lived experiences of others. Discomfort is a part of that process. The awareness that comes from this process will turn into action, advocacy, and sometimes even activism.

Help students understand white privilege in a nondefensive way. White privilege often makes students (and teachers) feel anxious or guilty, but if you are going to talk about race and racism, this has to be part of the discussion. Begin by focusing on the institutional facets of white privilege as opposed to labeling individual privilege. Showing students the big picture first can make discussions about our individual responsibilities much easier later on.

Focus on creating allyships. Take students through the discussion of what it means to be an ally. Show them what allyship looks like. Share your own stories of allyship. Invite your allies into your classroom or let them see the work others are also doing to dismantle racism. Fear will begin to subside when students know that they don't have to go it alone in working to create change.

If we don't work to create connections with and between students, we aren't fostering the development of learning environments that allow students to feel safe and valued. Not doing so can inhibit students from investing in their own learning and the learning of others. Education guru Rita Pierson is famous for her quote, "Kids don't learn from people they don't like," and she is right. I would also argue kids won't learn in a classroom with others they don't like. We've got to find ways, in all things, to show kids we care and to help them foster a love for one another. If we don't do this, how can we possibly expect students to enjoy coming to our classrooms to learn every day?

Reflecting on Your Practice

- What steps could you or do you already take to ensure you are building strong relationships with and between all students in your classroom?
- What do you feel is the most significant factor involved in building positive relationships with your students?

- What strategies do you or could you use to begin establishing a culture of antiracism in your classroom? In what ways might you support students in developing an awareness of racism so they are able to develop empathy and an understanding of the challenges of others who may be different from themselves?

ESSENTIAL PRACTICE #8: ESTABLISH A BELL-TO-BELL LEARNING ENVIRONMENT

Ask any teacher and they will tell you that time is one of the most valuable commodities they have because of its inherently limited nature. From morning and afternoon announcements to absenteeism to kids getting pulled out of our classrooms for a variety of reasons, everyday distractions snatch more and more learning time away from our students. Because of this, it's important that we take advantage of every second we have with students. This means learning should begin the very moment students arrive and should continue until our time together comes to an end. Practicing bell-to-bell learning gives students the opportunity to participate in a structured environment in which they can spend time learning both independently and collaboratively with one another for the duration of the time they are in our classrooms. Planning for bell-to-bell learning involves the development of engaging and rigorous lessons that serve all students, so kids remain motivated to learn from start to finish.

Take caution, however: bell-to-bell learning does not equate to the mundane provision of direct instruction for the duration of a class period, not even for the entirety of a single learning segment. Instead, learning bell to bell means having a diverse array of learning experiences and activities readily available for a variety of learner types so that learning is not just continuous but also continuously engaging!

Bell-to-bell learning is the foundational practice that creates the actual learning environment that is your classroom. It is the one practice that all other practices reside within. Bell-to-bell classrooms *are* the waters in which learning is navigated; where we ask students challenging questions; where we talk the talk of learning; where we assess, give feedback, and build relationships with our students. In the bell-to-bell classroom, your job as your students' guide throughout the learning process is indispensable.

When you implement bell-to-bell learning, you will be there to lead students toward understanding from the minute they show up until the time they leave you, each and every day. Because we know our students work at different paces and perform at different ability levels, bell-to-bell learning requires work on our part. Teachers must be prepared with lessons and activities that meet the needs of all learners, the kind that give students control of their own learning. Bell-to-bell learning also means taking the time to design engaging extension and enrichment activities versus simply providing more or extra work for fast finishers or high achievers.

Bell-to-bell learning involves students who are hard at work, rather than being kept busy with work, and this will look different in every classroom. In some classrooms bell-to-bell learning looks like students with heads down and hands furiously writing. In others, it is clusters of students gathered around a computer, problem-solving together. In others still, it is students sitting in a circle engaged in questioning, or taking notes while others perform or present to the rest of the class, or it may simply be the individual act of independent reading. In bell-to-bell classrooms, teachers are moving about the room, facilitating conversation, giving feedback, and doing all of the other things educators do while keeping students focused on learning. You are there for support and to make engagement easy for them.

Strategies for Implementation

Model the behavior you desire.

It is important for students to understand that expectations for learning in your classroom mean learning begins when the bell rings. You can model this by being ready yourself. Have your presentation materials on your e-board or projector before kids arrive. Have materials ready to pass out to students and do so as they get settled. You might even ask for a helper to do this for you. Get students engaged quickly by showing them you are ready to begin, so they should get ready, too.

Encourage students to prepare for learning.

As students arrive, greet them at the door and encourage them to get their resources and materials ready for learning. This means asking them to get out writing materials, start up their electronic devices, put away unnecessary items, or maybe even find a learning partner. When you build this kind of encouragement into your daily routine, students will come to understand that class time is invaluable, and they will always be ready to begin as soon as the bell rings!

Stay active in the classroom.

When students are hard at work, you should be, too! As much as possible, move around the room. As students work alone or together, drop by their desks to see how they are progressing. Ask questions about what they are doing and how they are doing it. Discuss problems and solutions by encouraging students to share their challenges as well as their success. Be cautious, though. Having busy students means time will pass quickly. Keep moving, but also keep an eye on the clock. Time in bell-to-bell classrooms flies by and will be gone before you know it!

Integrate bell-ringers and exit slips into your lesson plans.

Bell-ringers and exit slips are simply a way of kicking off learning and then buttoning it up. Asking students questions before introducing content requires them to dig into background knowledge and can get them engaged before any new material is even introduced. Do not skip this step when constructing lesson plans and class activities and be purposeful when adding bell-ringers and exit slips to your design for student learning. In your lesson plan template, carve out time and be stingy with it! When you consistently choose engaging questions to launch learning, students will come to appreciate the sense of curiosity these questions generate.

Because bell-to-bell learning requires educators to develop well-coordinated and differentiated lessons, this practice inherently aids teachers in overcoming the challenge of keeping students' attention. Twenty-first-century students are continuously distracted by day-to-day school activities, cell phones, school-issued devices, conversations with friends, and even "unsanctioned" daydreaming or sleeping during class. Bell-to-bell learning is a deterrent to these kinds of distractions. In classrooms that operate bell to bell, behavior is better, engagement is enhanced, maximum growth occurs, and at-risk students don't risk getting left behind. Bell-to-bell learning benefits everyone in the classroom.

While students spend time learning bell to bell, you should share in the enthusiasm you wish for them to have while they learn with you. That's right, I said *with you*. I learn something new from my students every day, and I tell them when I do. I want them to feel empowered by the fact that they can teach others, too. Even though there are days when students will receive instruction that comes directly from me, I want students to see me as a partner in their growth.

When we take steps to apply the first seven practices of the Essential Eight, bell-to-bell learning tends to occur naturally. It becomes an inherent part of what you and your students do together in a day.

Reflecting on Your Practice

- Think about what the beginning, middle, and end of your classes look and sound like now. Explain the impact this might have on learning.
- If you do not currently practice bell-to-bell learning, what would you need to change about your current teaching practice to be able to fully implement it in your classroom?
- Jot down an idea for a bell-ringer and an exit slip that you could use the next time you meet with students.

CLEARING THE PATH FOR ANTIRACIST LEARNING ENVIRONMENTS

In order to develop a clear plan for creating antiracist learning environments, educators must ask themselves three questions before getting started:

Is My Curriculum Fostering Learning through an Antiracist Lens?

Antiracist teaching and learning involves engaging students in various types of inquiry that first serve to answers two questions:

- How do structural *and* systemic racism impact the conditions and circumstances of others?
- How do my own individual actions and attitudes affect the conditions and circumstances of others?

To be able to help students answer these questions, we have to conduct an in-depth analysis of our curriculum. We must look for entry points into the curriculum where we can invite students to explore varying types of racism within the context of our content in order to bring students to an awareness of realities of racism. If our curriculum does not allow for this, we have to modify it such that it instead offers students diverse learning experiences that reinforce antiracist attitudes. Ours should become a curriculum that moves students toward the kind of awareness that brings about both individual and systemic change.

Does My Curriculum Encourage or Discourage Color Blindness?

When planning learning, we should be proactive in bringing students to content that is rich with color and culture. The voices within our content should be diverse. The learning experiences we present should offer students a glimpse at the lives of others who are different from our students in every way, from the foods they eat to the religions they follow. Be wary of using "we are all the same" language illogically as your platform for promoting antiracism in the classroom. We are all different, and that reality should be embraced, explored, exploited even, for the sake of teaching students that we must learn to value every individual and see them for exactly as the human beings they are in the color of the skin they are in.

Am I Prepared to Handle Controversial Topics When They Arise?

Controversial topics are inherently embedded within antiracist learning, and you must understand that these issues are at the core of some students' lived experiences. This is no reason to avoid them, however. The truth of the matter is, some students' lives literally hinge on the kind of understanding that comes from allowing students to engage in these conversations. Emotions may run high, so a key practice is to teach students how to engage in challenging conversations, how to show courage and respect, but also how to clearly articulate their thoughts, feelings, and emotions in a nonthreatening way. These are life skills, and we must help students learn to do this. If we don't know how to do this ourselves, it is imperative that we also learn.

If you were to ask my students, they would tell you that in my classroom we focus on learning about what matters to them. Yes, this still entails their learning to become skilled readers and writers, but the truth of the matter is, those things aren't necessarily interesting to all students. This practical framework for implementing the learning experiences you've designed can bring a renewed energy and excitement to learning. The only thing it doesn't provide is your own enthusiasm—that part is going to be up to you!

DROP ANCHOR

�֍ As you evaluate your current framework for teaching and learning, what nonnegotiables do you currently have in place? Where are you missing components of the Essential Eight as part of your daily practice?

✖ How might learning in your classroom change by implementing the Essential Eight in your daily instructional practice?

✖ Before your next learning segment, download the Essential Eight planning template from the *Plan Like a PIRATE* webpage at www.educationundone.com. Analyze your plans to make sure you have constructed learning that incorporates some or all of the PIRATE planning practices.

✖ After you have facilitated a learning segment that incorporates the Essential Eight, reflect on the impact to student engagement and learning. What did you notice about your classroom learning environment and the learners themselves?

✖ In order to determine if your curriculum allows students to work toward becoming actively antiracist, evaluate your content and your practice by exploring these three questions:

   ✖ Is my curriculum fostering learning through an antiracist lens?

   ✖ Does my curriculum encourage or discourage color blindness?

   ✖ Am I prepared to handle controversial topics when they arise?

SIX

PIRATE PLANNING IN ACTION

Teaching is a creative profession, not a delivery system.
Great teachers do [pass on information], but what great
teachers also do is mentor, stimulate, provoke, engage.

—SIR KEN ROBINSON

*P*IRATE teachers are always focused on taking their practice to the next level. PIRATE planning is the mechanism that guarantees our ability to kick our teaching up a notch via the beautifully crafted learning plans we design to meet the needs of every learner in our classrooms. PIRATE planning allows educators to create pathways for students to tap into the people, places, and things that matter to them. When we do this for our students, they will wholly commit to the learning process because that learning has real meaning to them.

The awesome thing about PIRATE planning is that you can apply it in every single learning segment you design. Each method, strategy, or practice has its own distinct features and purpose, and they can be easily joined with others to engineer awe-inspiring learning opportunities for every type of student. You might imagine yourself using them in the same way you would create with Lego bricks, for example. The building blocks of PIRATE planning are interchangeable and rely on the pieces above, below, and beside one another to ensure the effectiveness of those in between. By joining the right elements together, you are able to masterfully construct educational experiences that will leave your students on fire for learning and with memories that will last for years to come.

THE CREDO PROJECT

In early 2020, just before the COVID-19 pandemic devastatingly interrupted lives around the world, my English III students were engaged in a wonderful self-reflective, project-based learning activity I had designed just for them. It began as a way to prepare them for the English and reading portions of the ACT; however, long after the ACT was done, students still sought to engage with this uniquely individualized project that provided them an outlet to share their own wisdom and life advice with others. From this project, students learned not just to grab hold of the power of understanding language and the written word as tools for success, but more importantly, many of them developed a love for writing as they connected deeply with their inner selves by exploring the values that guide them through each day of their lives. The Credo Project, as I refer to it, is a model of PIRATE planning in action. This is a snapshot of my students' journey.

Anchors Aweigh

To launch the Credo Project, I began by talking with students about values. At first some struggled with the concept of possessing values. Even at the high school level, students immediately connected the word *value* to the idea of something having monetary worth. Allowing students to analyze the question "What does it mean to possess values?" via open dialogue and with emphasis on the pluralization of the word eventually brought some clarity. As their guide, I dropped hints and questions that led students on a path to discovery: "Have you heard the phrase *moral values*?" or "How do our values affect our day-to-day decisions?" and "What does it mean when a person has no values?"

This search for understanding gave me the opening to ask students to begin their own inquiry. I concluded our discussion with a simple task: "Take out a sheet of paper. I want you to begin making a list of the values you feel you possess. Choose one or two and briefly explain how embracing these values has affected your life."

Asking these kinds of personal, critical questions early in the project brought a high level of engagement and interest in learning because students immediately realized, *Hey, this is going to be about me, about my life.* Our conversation and the short constructed response made for a great kickoff of this student-centered, student-led unit that would involve experiences that were important and relevant to them.

The Credo Project officially began in January, when we returned from the holiday break and, in my original plan, would continue up until the ACT was administered in early February. We started the unit by looking at sample ACTs to see how students would be asked to engage with the questions, and together we examined the abundant academic language that existed within the test itself. This was primarily to give students familiarity with the test's format so that when they saw the examination on the actual test day, they would not be overwhelmed. For a week or so, we took a few minutes of each class to break apart the test. This was very important, and we did it in tandem with our daily engagement in the project. I also did a bit of diagnostic assessment because I wanted to gauge, mid-year, where students were with the language and grammar skills we had explored up until December. For this assessment, I used the online assessment tool Plickers, which is a fun way to have students provide multiple-choice responses without requiring them to have clickers or computers. Using your phone or tablet, all you have to do is scan rotatable QR-code cards as students hold them up, and voila! The feedback is instant.

After I had the data I needed, we discussed how the English portion of the ACT asks students to demonstrate understanding of concepts like proper use of grammar, sentence structure, punctuation, and rhetorical style. The reading portion requires students to analyze and evaluate a multitude of texts such as prose fiction, informational texts, and other narrative types. While these are all skills we had worked to improve throughout the previous semester, it was now time to make sure students had grasped them, and I wasn't going to do that by giving them "drill and kill" sample tests over and over again. Although I wanted to make sure they had the stamina to complete the test, I also did not want to burn them out before they had taken it. So, what did we do? We reviewed all of the skills they needed right within the Credo Project.

Our earlier exploration of the word *values* had already set the stage for the learning that was about to occur and had highlighted the need to study language in the context. As we carried out our discussion in class, we used academic language such as *analyze* and *explain*, but we had really begun our learning journey with the word *values*, a domain-specific word, as the basis for the anticipatory discussion used to introduce the Credo Project.

The Importance of Language Study in Context

The acquisition of language in context, whether academic or domain-specific vocabulary, is essential to enduring understanding. We must never simply give students words and expect them to be instantly internalized. Instead, we must allow students to develop relationships with words and learn to create connections between themselves and language so that it can be easily retrieved and applied when needed. Analyzing language in the context of students' own lives—as we did in the beginning of this project—gave students the chance to do just that: make language connections to promote retention. Words like *analyze*, *explain*, and *values* might have been words students encountered on the ACT, but even if they didn't, they were still building relationships with these words, and many others, as they examined them via this project. In the event students needed these words in other areas of study, now or later in their lives, they would be readily accessible and easily applied.

The great thing about approaching language in this way is that students will begin to care about words when you show them how to use them in their own voice to express their own ideas. They will gain confidence because they have learned to use language in ways that will help them convey exactly what they want to say. They will care about how their words read, how they look, and how they sound when they use them. Now, when a student is asked to "analyze" something, they can easily refer back to the time they had to analyze their own values. If they are asked to "share their values," they will know how to do this easily because they've explored them previously. Establishing connections between academic and content vocabulary beneath the umbrella of students' own experiences is extremely important to lasting understanding.

To further assist us in our study of language and grammar, we adopted Strunk and White's *The Elements of Style* as our writing guide, which we also used in conjunction with a number of Pear Deck collaborative activities. Pear Deck is a fabulous online resource that allows educators to brilliantly transform Google Slides into engaging, interactive learning experiences that reveal, in real time, where each student is in their learning. Using reconstructed examples from Strunk and White inserted into Pear Deck presentations, I gave students the opportunity, in groups, to evaluate whether or not language and grammar were used correctly in my own "revised" excerpts from the text. In addition to this, students created and participated in their own language-centered escape room activities, and I had them proofread everything they put their hands on. Believe me, teenagers get a kick out of being able to find other people's errors! This grammar and language practice and review was done concurrently with all other parts of the project, putting knowledge and skills to use in the context of every bit of content we explored.

"Mrs. Harris, What Is a Credo?"

Along with *The Elements of Style*, we also cracked open a brand-new classroom set of Robert Fulghum's best-selling essay collection titled

All I Really Need to Know I Learned in Kindergarten. In this entertaining and original collection, Fulghum leads readers on a journey to understanding through brief essays about all things related to being human. Readers are pulled in by Fulghum's writing style that is sometimes funny, sometimes awe-inspiring, sometimes sorrowful—but that always invites us to examine our lives through each of his unique ponderings.

Because the book's title essay is often referred to as Fulghum's credo, I had students explore the word *credo* by asking them to search the web for a definition. We settled on Google's dictionary definition: "a statement of the beliefs or aims which guide someone's actions." We then took a close look at Fulghum's title essay and analyzed it to see if it lived up to the definition of a credo, and the answer was a clear yes. We then took time to read through several of his other essays over a few days, and through questioning and discussion, students realized that all his written pieces connected in some way to his original credo. Every single thing he wrote seemed to tie back to his learnings from kindergarten. It was amazing to watch students make these connections and discover the deliberate nature of Fulghum's writing that would help us all learn something about ourselves. Little did they know, they would soon be doing the very same thing: crafting their credos to inspire and lift up others.

On a side note, because all the while we had been busy exploring language in context, students were thrilled when they found Fulghum's book contained many grammar errors and typos. They were actually pleading to contact the publisher! Instead, we talked about how important it is to generate quality work. Because they had identified errors in a book that had sold over 7 million copies, many of them thought, *Couldn't they produce better-quality writing than this if they were the ones finding the errors?* Their confidence soared and their minds raced. *They could be million-copy best sellers, too!* They were revved up to begin their journey to authordom.

The Journey Before Them

From our exploration of the term *credo*, students then constructed their own credos in just a few simple steps:

- They first created mind maps that incorporated every facet of their individual values and beliefs.
- Students used their mind maps to construct one-sentence personal belief statements that would serve as their credo statement.
- They utilized their statements, just as Robert Fulghum did, as the basis for an essay in which they explained their credo in just a few pages.
- Once their credos were as polished as they could be, students peer edited using what they had learned from our previous language study. (I referred to this as "real-world application of skills." Students were all-in, so to speak, and did some of the highest-quality peer editing I have ever seen.)

Little did my students know that the essays they crafted were just the beginning of what would be an ongoing collection of writing that would be housed on a web-based platform so they could share their stories and voices with others. These authentic and deeply personal messages would serve as the cornerstones for personal blogs that would eventually be filled with as much writing and as many creative and personal pieces as their hearts desired!

From Blog to Test

While most students were familiar with podcasts and vlogging—YouTube vlogs, in particular—many of them weren't sure what blogs were or what they were designed to do. While some students declared blogging an activity for "old people," once we analyzed a variety of blogs, many came to see the value in their content, on both a personal and a professional level. We discussed blogging as an important life skill that would allow them to practice real-world writing and communication skills. Through this discussion, students realized their work here would result in them becoming published authors on a real-world platform. When asked how a blog might further help them, they suggested that their work could be utilized later for college entrance essays, résumé enhancers, or writing samples for employers or universities.

To begin the blogging process, once students' credo statements were finished, we again took a look at a number of blogs, beginning with Robert Fulghum's, which is titled *Journal Entries*. This simplistic titling was beneficial as it helped students to better understand another purpose for blogging, in a nutshell. We read several examples of Fulghum's posts and compared the themes to those present in his book. Students were able to connect the language and messaging in Fulghum's posts to much of what was in his book (right down to more errors!). Through this activity, students continued to demonstrate their readiness for the ACT via their involvement in this evaluative and analytical process. It was fascinating to watch them learn and grow through the examination of the written words of others, as well as their own.

Next, students generated their blogs using Google Sites, a simplistic tool for creating blogs quickly that doesn't require students to be highly skilled at setting up or manipulating a website from scratch. We did this in about one class period. Their credo statement and essay would be the main page of their site and would greet everyone who entered their blog.

Beyond the initial credo essay, students were required to develop three additional written blog posts that would also be peer edited for language, grammar, and style, after which they would post the final, edited versions to their Google Sites. I permitted students to add one additional piece to their blog in the format of their choosing. They could choose to record a podcast episode, create a piece of visual art, generate a vlog, write a poem or song lyrics, or share a collage of photos or images. As with all other pieces, the content had to be derived from their mind maps and connected to their credo essays or statements. They worked diligently to produce heartfelt pieces they were confident about sharing with the world. They knew their words were going to make a difference to someone, somewhere.

By early February, the students were ready to take the ACT. They had worked hard studying grammar and language in order to make their written publications exceptional, and they were *actively* demonstrating a command of the English language. They had learned to read and analyze the work of others—not just for content, but for style, usage, and understanding—all things they would be asked to do on the ACT. And when the test was done and they returned to me, I could tell they felt reassured. They were confident about what they had accomplished both in our classroom and on the examination. And most importantly, they wanted to continue their Credo Project work. My heart was overjoyed, but even better, my students' hearts (and minds) were on fire because of all they had accomplished!

PIRATE PLANNING IN THE CREDO PROJECT

I am a firm believer in the power of great teaching in the same way that I am dogmatic in my beliefs about the necessity of well-constructed, actionable plans for learning—plans that include showing students how to make the world a better place; plans that allow every student to be engaged; plans that are differentiated, that are antiracist, and that incorporate the Essential Eight each and every time.

The Credo Project captures all these things and demonstrates exactly what it means to plan like a PIRATE.

CHARTING THE COURSE TO A BETTER WORLD

Curiosity

From the outset of this unit, students were intrigued by the project as a whole. They were surprised to find that their teacher wanted to know what life advice *they* had to offer! Throughout our exploration of values and the sharing of stories, students naturally took an interest in learning more about one another. The small-group conversations students engaged in during peer-editing sessions sometimes led to more questions than feedback. They wanted to know more about blogging. They wanted to explore what all they could do with a website. And most of all, they wanted to know how they might craft a message as powerful as Robert Fulghum's. I can say with certainty, many of them did so. Their curiosity led to answers, their answers led to confidence, and their confidence led to success.

Hope

Another beautiful discussion that ensued in the early days of the project centered on the hopes and dreams of students and the views they held about their futures. They were going to take the ACT in a little over a month, so their minds began thinking about what it would mean if they did well or, conversely, if they did not. Some wondered if they would change their minds about going straight into the workforce if they did well on the ACT. Would they consider going to college instead then? I believe many students really grasped on to thinking differently about their future and what they could do with their lives regardless of the score they got on the ACT. This conversation was pivotal in their decision to take this process of growth seriously. Through the deep exploration of their lives this project brought them to, many students were also able to see how much they had grown and how their lives had changed for the better due to the hope and faith they had held onto so strongly over the years.

Advocacy

The story of "the self" is empowering. By revealing their stories via the Credo Project blog entries they created, students were able to use their voices to inform others of the struggles and obstacles they overcame to be able to enjoy the lives they led. When constructing their blog posts, students didn't just explain the challenges they had faced, but they demonstrated how those challenges impacted them, often forcing them to turn negatives into positives in order to survive emotionally. In many cases, students' stories involved beautiful examples of self-advocacy that they were able to translate into powerful messaging that would help others become empowered to advocate for themselves, too.

Responsibility

In the Credo Project, students learned what it means to have a responsibility to others. They learned it was important to show up for others when it was time to give feedback and to actively listen so they could provide honest, meaningful input even through something like peer editing. They realized that their stories have power, and when they are comfortable doing so, they can use those stories to help others. Responsibility to oneself was also in play when students committed their time, effort, and energy to fully engaging with the learning so they could improve their skills, whether it was because they wanted to do well on the ACT, become a skilled communicator, or both.

Tolerance

The writing students constructed in this project was far from the informational or argumentative five-paragraph essays they were accustomed to. Instead, this narrative storytelling focused specifically on students' lives and experiences that helped shape them into the people they had become now. By sharing their stories, students learned much about one another, the differences and similarities between their families, their cultures, and their values. Exposure to these stories helped to foster empathy and create a deeper sense of community in our classroom. Sharing their identities helped students open up to ways of life and belief systems they might not have accepted previously. This project inherently fostered attitudes of tolerance and acceptance as it opened students' eyes to the fact that we aren't really as different as we seem.

THE VESSEL FOR ENGAGEMENT

Broadening Access to Information via Technology

I explained to students at the outset of this project that their learning experiences were going to rely heavily on the use of technology. For example, the activities and assessments students engaged in were assigned and graded in Google Classroom; students used private comments to communicate about questions both during and outside of class; they used Google Calendar to track due dates; and students created stunning blogs with Google Sites. Establishing the procedures and methods for digitally accessing information and for interacting with one another at the outset of the unit helped to eliminate confusion and left students feeling confident about how to navigate their own learning via technology.

An Outside-the-Box Learning Experience

The Credo Project was itself a reimagining of learning in that it asked students to engage in a nontraditional process for expanding their knowledge and skills related to English language arts content. Inviting students to learn through a real-world experience, in this case maintaining a personal blog, offered a unique approach to bringing students to new understanding about language and in a much more exciting way than the standard test prep so many of them were accustomed to enduring. The Credo Project turned learning about language on its head as it challenged students to see the value of understanding language because it gave them a voice with which they could help others. When students grasped this and experienced the power language holds, they wanted to do better. They wanted their language skills to be phenomenal.

Time for Pausing to Regroup

This was an extensive unit with many moving parts and pieces. Students were responsible for utilizing technology, reading literature, examining parts of the ACT, studying language and grammar concurrent with exploring content, and learning to blog, all while digging deeply into their own personal stories and experiences. They were invested fully and working hard. There were days, though, when I knew my kiddos needed a break.

On one afternoon in particular, after students had settled into their project work, a student jokingly mentioned that she was tired because she had spent too much time the night before watching Primitive Builder videos on YouTube. If you aren't familiar with these videos, they feature individuals who have abandoned current technology and, instead, rely solely on primitive tools to create elaborate dwellings dug by hand and constructed with handmade bricks. Many of these creations have beautifully landscaped pools or remarkable outdoor entertainment areas. They are a sight to see for sure, especially considering that they involve zero use of modern tools or machinery! Upon mention of the videos, several students commented that they had never seen one before, and so the begging began: "Please, Mrs. Harris, please can we watch just one!" In this case, students weren't explicitly telling me they needed a break, but I sensed they could use one. How could I say no?

As we watched one of the videos, we discussed the autonomous sensory meridian response (ASMR) elements of the videos and their effect on the viewer; we discussed the authenticity of the videos and the work itself, as in, what was taking place that we couldn't see; we talked about the moral dilemma the videos posed, as we weren't entirely sure the builders were getting the recognition they deserved. (Students did find out later that one group of builders had received an award from YouTube for their millions of views—they were extremely happy to hear that!)

The end of our video session brought us back to our task as we concluded with a quick discussion question that tied back to our Credo Project work: What life advice might the primitive builders have to offer? This offered a great segue back into exploring their own life advice. Students were recharged and ready to get back on track. This brief fifteen-minute diversion gave them just the pause they needed to regroup!

SAILING THE SEAS OF DIFFERENTIATION

High Planning

To determine where students needed the most support, I used ACT practice and academic vocabulary diagnostic assessments. After assessing the results of the practice ACT, I realized students were struggling most with sentence structure. The data allowed me to see which students needed the most support as well as where my highest learners could work to improve.

The Plickers diagnostic assessment gave a snapshot of academic language literacy as it stood at that point in the school year. I added a few more challenging words to see the limit of students' knowledge and was able to use that data to determine where some students struggled and where others soared. Once it had been analyzed, this assessment data became the basis from which all tiered learning targets were developed for the overarching unit.

On a side note, these two assessments were administered prior to and completely independent of the unit. I did not share with students that this data would be used for anything until I had analyzed it and until the learning targets were defined. While I was working on evaluating this assessment data, students began their reading of the unit text, *All I Really Need to Know I Learned in Kindergarten*.

Deep Planning

The project's overarching learning targets were based on observational and diagnostic assessment data and tiered according to each learning group's needs:

Tier 3: By examining Robert Fulghum's essay collection, students will be able to **analyze** their own real-life experiences or events and incorporate them into complex ideas and concepts by **creating and maintaining a personal, narrative blog** in which they effectively use precise language, domain-specific vocabulary, and varied sentence structure as well as figurative language techniques such as metaphor, simile, and analogy to enhance blog content.

Tier 2: By examining Robert Fulghum's essay collection, students will be able to **analyze** their own real-life experiences or events and **translate them into unique written perspectives** by **creating and maintaining a personal, narrative blog** in which they effectively use precise language, domain-specific vocabulary, and correct sentence structure to enhance blog content.

Tier 1: By examining Robert Fulghum's essay collection, students will be able to **recall** their own real-life experiences or events in order to **describe the effect** these had on their lives by **creating and maintaining a personal, narrative blog** in which they effectively use domain-specific vocabulary and correct sentence structure to enhance blog content.

Note: As is always the case, to further support differentiated learning experiences, students engaged with a number of supporting learning targets tied to mini-lessons throughout the project's duration. All learning targets were developed ahead of learning and provided foundations for learning based on students' needs. Not every student engaged with every supporting learning target, but every student engaged with at least some of the learning targets throughout the unit plan.

Wide Planning

In every way, the Credo Project was a fully inclusive, student-centered experience. Throughout the process, students spent a considerable amount of time asking and answering questions. They wanted to know all about blogging (to be honest, many of them had never even seen, let alone read one). They wondered how Robert Fulghum had become an author and why his book has sold so many copies. They were curious about how their peers were approaching the blog project. So many questions, so many answers.

Students also spent considerable time reflecting on their work, what they had written and how their own individual experiences strengthened their stories. They shared their deeply emotional stories, funny stories, memorable moments—all of which had helped shape the people they had become. They were excited to share those stories with their peers, and through that experience, our class became even closer than it already was.

Students worked in groups periodically throughout the unit, particularly when we engaged in new learning. The data that I captured from the diagnostic assessments at the outset of the unit not only helped me to establish the learning targets but also helped me with intentionally grouping students so that every working group had at least one student from each of the tier one, tier two, and tier three groups. When we engaged in exercises like escape rooms, Pear Deck team activities, and "pass the folder" vocabulary activities where students collaborated during timed sessions to competitively practice language skills, each group worked together as a fully functioning unit with its very own system of support built in—the highest-performing students built empathy, leadership, and teamwork skills, and students needing the most support never once felt "less than."

BECOMING ANTIRACIST

Building Culture and Understanding

Because this project was filled to the brim with every facet of students' identities at play, we shared a lot about our personal lives and selves. In one of my Credo Project classrooms, one student was Black biracial, just like me. When the student shared information about their lived experiences inside and outside of school, students were naturally curious. The class actually had many questions for both me and their peer as biracial individuals, and at this point in the year, we were both okay with answering those questions because we had worked hard to create a beautiful culture of belonging in which every student felt valued. We could answer their questions because we felt safe doing so.

During some of our moments of pause, students would curiously inquire about how we cared for our hair, what our families were like, or how our food and culture was different than their own, but we also learned about theirs at the same time. When they asked, we asked. The students even commented about how this student and I could pass for mother and child since we had the same skin, the same big brown eyes and long, curly hair. We also talked about how the same could be said for non-people of color in the building and how it's important to look for nuances in every person's physical and intellectual traits, which will allow us to see so much more in individuals than we ever did at first. It was a beautiful learning experience for everyone involved. It would have been easy to shy away from these discussions, but we did not. Our conversations were a deeply transformative exercise in building relationships and fostering empathy and antiracist attitudes.

NAVIGATING THE CREDO PROJECT WITH THE ESSENTIAL EIGHT

Concept-Based Learning

The entire focus of the Credo Project centered upon the idea that we can use a blog as a vehicle for telling our personal stories so that we can help others who may be struggling to figure out their own lives. Through this concept-based unit of study, students learned to develop skills related to language use, sentence structure, clarification of ideas, and constructing written responses for publication.

Critical Thinking and Inquiry

Students posed their own questions to me and to their peers throughout the learning process. These were only a few of the questions we explored:

- What are values, and how do mine influence the kind of person I am?
- What life experiences do I share with others? How can my lived experiences help others who may be struggling in similar ways as I have?
- How does my ability to communicate effectively, orally and in writing, help me to convey ideas I feel strongly about?
- How does one become a published writer?
- What is the purpose of blogging?
- How does my ability to use language affect my success in life?

Academic and Domain-Specific Vocabulary

Through diagnostic assessment, I identified the academic language students needed the most support to develop a command of use. Throughout the project, when these words arose, we stopped to discuss them. In our documentation, these words were bold and underlined wherever they appeared.

The domain-specific content vocabulary came directly from the focal point of our studies: the blogging process, the language of sentence structure learning, and from Robert Fulghum's collection of essays.

Academic	Domain-Specific
Analyze, Evaluate, Infer, Assess, Judge, Examine, Explain, Interpret, Formulate, Defend, Contrast	Credo, Values, Blog, Attitude, Perspective, Cynical, Naive, The Golden Rule, Existential, Extrapolate, Fundamental, Distillation, Compound, Complex, Compound-Complex

Purposeful Use of Technology

Students were never without an opportunity to purposefully interact with technology throughout this project. From Plickers as a form of diagnostic assessment to Pear Deck to facilitate learning related to sentence structure, technology provided both the means for assessment and the outlet for showing mastery of skills. Google Sites was a tool for giving students voice, and Google Docs allowed students not only to write their personal stories but also to gather constructive feedback from their peers. Technology in the Credo Project did not merely replace traditional tools for learning; it advanced students' capabilities of demonstrating mastery at an exceptional level.

Constructed Response Daily

From day one of this project, students were immersed in writing. They took part in reflective written responses to Robert Fulghum's essays and blog posts. They engaged in daily writing sessions as they worked to construct their own blog posts, and they regularly provided digital and handwritten feedback to their peers. The Credo Project focused on helping students to establish themselves as authors, and as with any endeavor such as this, practice makes perfect. And practice they did . . . every single day.

Meaningful, High-Quality Feedback

To ensure students remained on track toward their goals, students and I participated in one-on-one teacher feedback sessions at least once per week to discuss their stories and to allow them to share how they felt they were progressing. In peer-to-peer feedback sessions, students provided input on other students' blog posts and ideas. Peer-editing sessions allowed students to evaluate one another's grammar skills and writing structure before final publication to their blogs. Because this project would result in published material, students wanted meaningful feedback. They were wide open to it and applied it in ways that made them better writers and their published pieces more powerful.

Strong Relationships

This entire project was an exercise in relationship building. Through the sharing of their stories, the bond between students grew stronger. Students spent time in small groups, and the relationships in those groups grew as well. We were closer as a class because of this project. What students shared were some of the most vulnerable moments of their lives, but they shared them anyway because they trusted and valued one another. It was beautiful to witness their openness and the sense of community that emerged.

Bell-to-Bell Learning

Once the project details had been shared with the group and students learned that any and all activities related to the Credo Project were categorically organized under the same heading in Google Classroom, students knew exactly where to look for materials, instructions, due dates, and more. Students were engaged in self-paced work. The learning environment ran itself. Sure, there were days when we paused to reenergize or engaged in new learning segments together, but the class operated as a self-sufficient learning machine. That didn't mean, however, that students didn't ask me or their peers questions. Self-advocacy is something we talked about from the very beginning in our classroom, so when kids needed help, they asked for it. They were motivated, energized, overflowing with passion and a commitment to this project because it was theirs—their stories, their words, their hearts on full display so others could learn from their experiences. This was a bell-to-bell experience in every way.

THE LIGHTING OF A FIRE

This project was one of the most rewarding teaching experiences I've ever had the pleasure of guiding. I saw my students come to class each day on fire to get to work on their blogs. They wanted to tell their stories—no, they *needed* to tell them. Learning and hard work went hand in hand. Students knew that if they wanted their writing to have an impact on others, then the English "lessons" were a necessary part of that process. My job was to make those learning experiences as engaging and student centered as possible. Students collaborated and bounced their ideas off one another. They were on a quest for feedback—they wanted it from me, and they wanted it from their peers. They wanted their blogs to be perfect. And, in my opinion, they were.

Planning in this way is magical, for you and for students. It's like putting a match to fuel, and once the fire is set, there is no putting it out. Students had complete control of their learning, and they were committed and determined to learn every skill and understand every concept in order to make their stories unforgettable. The task of preparing to succeed on the ACT was secondary. The important task, they felt, was to provide advice to others based on their own experiences, and they would do whatever was necessary to be able to do that well. Reaching the ACT score they desired was simply a by-product of all they had done. The Credo Project is an example of what happens when we take the time and steps to create learning opportunities that are engaging, student centered, and tailored to every student's needs. This is PIRATE planning at its core.

DROP ANCHOR

- As you begin the transition to PIRATE planning, what might you need to change about the way you plan now in order to design the kind of learning that sets students' hearts and minds on fire for learning?
- Which of the Essential Eight practices do you use most often? Least often? How might you redefine your existing lesson plans to ensure that the Essential Eight are part of your daily instruction?
- What are you doing now to ensure you are creating an inclusive, antiracist culture in your classroom? How do you focus on relationship building to ensure empathy and tolerance are inherently developed in the interactions you design for students?

PART IV

Be It

OWN YOUR SUCCESS

SEVEN

Power Up Your Professionalism

The most valuable resource that all teachers have is each other. Without collaboration our growth is limited to our own perspectives.
—ROBERT JOHN MEEHAN

I think we can all agree that the people with whom we spend our time have the power to impact our lives tremendously, both positively and negatively. This is true whether we're talking about our families, our friendships, romantic relationships, and even our professional connections. Because our job as educators is to serve kids in every way, we cannot afford to surround ourselves with others who don't help to elevate us in this task. Instead, we need others around us who can help us through the struggles in our work and who bring out the best in us, so we can be our best for kids. Being part of a PLC as well as a PLN is vital to every educator's success, both in and beyond the classroom. The observable differences in the levels of passion, enthusiasm, and growth of educators involved in professional circles and collaboratives compared to that of educators who are not is quite significant. When we join together with the right kind of people, educators can accomplish almost anything, and we most definitely can *be* whatever it is we wish to become.

FIND YOUR PEOPLE, FIND YOUR PURPOSE

Near the end of my teaching program many years ago, one of my professors engaged our class in a discussion surrounding the idea that classroom teaching may be just one leg of our journey in education. We discussed the many opportunities we may be presented with throughout our careers: education administration, higher education, government or private-sector work, educational entrepreneurship, training and professional development—the possibilities were endless.

When our discussion was over, I distinctly remember asking my professor how she had been able to turn her own passion into the specialized professional education work she was doing at that time. She quickly replied, "Don't worry, you'll figure out what you were meant to do one day. You'll know where you're supposed to be when the time comes." I won't ever forget that moment. Perplexed by her response, I managed to squeeze out a confused "thank you," and our would-be conversation ended as abruptly as it had begun. It was clear that my professor understood my question, but her reply made no sense to me. Maybe she was in a hurry. Maybe she just didn't feel like answering. Either way, I walked away with even more questions.

After years of wondering where my career in education would take me and attempting to identify my role in helping to shape the lives of the students I serve, I believe I finally found my own answer to that puzzling question of purpose.

To discover your purpose in this vast field of education, you first need to seek out those like yourself who share the same fire for education. Find those who will lift you up, but who will also challenge you. Find others who love kids and education as much as you do. Find people with whom you can share your gifts and vice versa. Observe the impact of those leading with passion, those who are fearless visionaries.

Find those who understand the power of the collective to transform education and become part of that collective. When you find people like this, join them, because they will help guide you toward your calling in this vast profession. Sadly, it took me more years than I care to mention to come to this understanding on my own.

You see, when we seek to become part of a network of education professionals on fire for education, we expose ourselves to the many ways in which educators are leaving their mark on the world. Passionate, purpose-driven educators are everywhere, and they are looking for others to engage in the work of transforming education right alongside them. Not only will their contributions help us remain laser-focused on our own mission and goals, but they will also teach us, inspire us, lead us, and empower us to keep pressing forward even in the most challenging of times.

In education, we have two choices: we can be observers of and sometimes even contributors to the problems that exist in education, or we can be part of the solutions necessary to fix those problems. Our decision can be career changing for us, but more importantly, it can be life changing for kids. The sooner we find our people, the sooner we will discover our purpose and can set about changing education and, in effect, the lives of children.

ENGAGING IN A CULTURE OF COLLABORATION WITH YOUR PLC

If student growth and achievement are important to you, your professional learning community should be, too. Your PLC is the body of educators with whom you may spend considerable time collaborating, mapping out curriculum, analyzing assessment data, attending teacher-based team meetings, and more. They are the educators in your department or grade level working directly with you to ensure that the structure of learning is effective and aligns with the mission and vision of your school. This group might also include department chairs, instructional coaches, curriculum directors, administrators, intervention specialists, and even parents or caregivers. When we talk about decision-making and protocols for learning as it directly pertains to our students, our PLC is the body representing the stakeholders who *are* our students.

Hopefully, you are blessed to belong to a high-functioning PLC. For those of us who are, we know the power that group of leaders holds to create a dynamic school experience for teachers and for kids. Our collective knowledge, experiences, beliefs, values, and insights, when brought together, offer us so much to dissect when we think about what it means to educate kids, and every bit of that collective wisdom is valuable to decision-making. That doesn't mean, though, that every PLC is going to operate smoothly and without conflict or differences in opinion. When things get difficult, it's always best to take a moment to pause and realize one very important thing: every suggestion, every piece of advice, every idea, no matter how much we disagree, is coming from another person who, like you, has students' best interest at heart. When we realize this, it's much easier to approach our differences with level heads. Our work may feel personal, but nothing we decide in our PLC is about us. It never has been, and it never will be. It is about students, plain and simple. With that in mind, decision-making and disagreements become much easier to navigate.

IT IS ABOUT STUDENTS, PLAIN AND SIMPLE

There are so many things we can do together with our PLC even outside of mandated activities. We might design cotaught lessons, establish intervention protocols, create units of study, determine how we will use data to best meet an individual student's needs, or equally as important, plan fun activities for students and staff to engage in together. For example, one year at Halloween, a group of teachers and students in our building coordinated a choreographed pass-time performance in costume to Michael Jackson's "Thriller"! It was an amazing four minutes of fun that gave us all something to talk and laugh about for a long time after. When we collaborate and plan together with our PLC, we are not only actively engaging in our own growth process, but we are building both relationships and designs for learning that have the potential to transform school for kids.

Do be sure to find time for more than just work in your PLC. Celebrate your accomplishments as a team recognizing all the hard work you have done. Plan to attend out-of-school conferences together. Take time to do fun things like going for cocktails on an evening before a break, or plan an outing after school to go golfing, crafting, or get in some self-care at the spa or gym! One of my favorite experiences in my teaching career came when I spent a weekend in Atlanta, GA, attending an education conference with members of my PLC. To this day, we still talk about the memories from that informative *and* entertaining experience! Remember, you and your PLC are a team, and your happiness and success can hinge on your effectiveness as one. Building relationships with one another is a critical step toward that.

YOUR SOCIAL MEDIA PLN AS A RESOURCE FOR PROFESSIONAL GROWTH

My online professional learning network has been absolutely vital to my growth and development as an education practitioner. I have been blessed to be able to learn from people around the world about the best strategies for reaching and supporting kids. My PLN has even helped me see strengths in my own practice I wasn't aware I possessed. They will become some of the best friends you've ever had, and you won't believe the impact on the world of education you will be able to make together, yet from afar—it's quite amazing!

Every social media platform brings new faces and new ways for educators to engage with one another, from Twitter chats and Facebook

Groups to Instagram Live broadcasts and Clubhouse drop-ins. Too often, though, social media gets a bad rap for the negativity that seems to outweigh the good that also dwells there. Negativity is everywhere and is something we can choose to subject ourselves to or not; just like in the real world, who you choose to surround yourself with online will have an impact on the level of joy and growth you experience there. You have choices you'll need to make about what kinds of connections you wish to form. Your PLN should provide you a safe space for sharing ideas and a platform for learning and growth that will bring you a new sense of excitement and confidence about your skills as an educator.

There's much at stake when we don't take advantage of the opportunities for growth that engaging with our PLN on social media offers us. Getting on the path to finding and growing with your own online PLN is much easier than you might think.

Create a Written Vision of the Teacher You Are or Wish to Become

Ask yourself what you envision accomplishing as an educator. Your journey to growth must begin with a clear vision, and having one means you will also have the power to greatly influence your students and others.

So before you hop on your favorite social media platform again, take a few minutes to jot down, in your journal or some other spot where you reflect, your thoughts about what you hope to accomplish as an educator. Articulate in your own words how you feel about your students and what you want for them. You might even write down some notes about your beliefs as they relate to the ways in which you carry out educating children. Doing this will help you as you engage in conversations with other educators about your own approach to teaching.

While having your own website or a blog isn't necessary, it may provide a place for your reflections and learning as you carry out your work in education. You might also consider using it as a place to compile what you have learned from both your PLC and your PLN. You can then reveal those learnings to others by sharing your blog posts on your favorite social media platform.

Since growth equals change—and with the help of your PLN, you will be growing—be prepared to periodically refine your vision and goals to reflect your evolution as an educator.

Develop More Than Just Your Profile—Create Your Image

Developing an online social media profile that captures the essence of your identity is so important. The image you project of yourself can bring you just the kinds of connections you are searching for. When other educators see your profile, they should learn at least one thing about you that would make them want to connect with you. Remember, your goal is to make helpful connections, not simply gather up followers. Having a dynamic profile will let others know what you are all about and that you'll be a great addition to their PLN.

On Twitter, for example, your banner and profile are like calling cards introducing you to the Twitter world. Consider art or photos that capture you as well as your interests. Pictures of your classroom are great, but also consider including imagery that embodies your beliefs and values. Think about what kinds of things might be symbolic of who you are as an educator. If you can, include text on your banner. For instance, if you have a website or blog, include your web address. Also include some of your favorite hashtags, or make up one of your own! This will easily let others know where your interests lie.

Your social media handle, often referred to as your @ symbol, might be tricky to choose. Many people like to get creative with their handles, and that's up to you if you choose to go this route. Just make sure people can still find you. It's okay if you want to use a nickname in your handle, but my advice is to make sure some part of your social media profile contains your name—if you want people to know your name, that is. Some educators choose not to include their real name for a variety of reasons, and that's okay, too.

Find the Experts, Follow Them, and Engage Fully

Begin growing your PLN by searching for your favorite authors, thought leaders, podcast hosts, or any other education experts you have sought to learn from in your work. After you follow them, don't worry if they don't follow you back right away, but also don't be surprised if they do! Most educators and leaders are extremely active in engaging with their followers. They are there to help because they understand that growth is a lifelong journey and they, too, want the opportunity to learn alongside others like you. Educators share on social media because they have something to say, and many will reply especially when it comes to topics related to kids and professional growth. So don't be afraid. Reach out! Once you have chosen a few people to follow, check your feed often to see what they are sharing.

Post Consistently and Reply Regularly

You began building your PLN when you made the decision to follow your favorite education leaders and their followers. Now that you have the roots of a solid PLN, it's time for you to begin sharing your own content! It's so easy to become an active voice on social media. Here are a few things you can do:

Ask a question. What do you want to know about or learn about? Someone will either answer you or point you in the right direction.

Drop a quote. Give people something to ponder. You'll surely get responses from your followers. This is one of the easiest ways to make connections. Everyone has a favorite quote that encourages, inspires, or motivates them!

Write a review or leave a link. Have you found something interesting on the world wide web? Share it! People will thank you.

Do you see where I'm going here? You have to take an active role in finding your people. If you don't let them know you exist, they can't respond and you can't develop relationships with them. And as all teachers know, developing relationships is the single best contributing factor to learning. We do this in our classrooms every day!

Do try to post or tweet consistently so people can see you're engaged. Your social media feed can be a busy place and people are choosy with notifications, so the more you post or share, the higher the likelihood people will want to connect with you. At the same time, don't post just for the sake of posting. You want your contributions to be authentic and to serve a greater purpose than to simply capture attention.

Also be sure to reply when people comment on your posts. It's the polite thing to do. When someone holds the door, you say, "Thank you." The same applies on social media. A little kindness goes a long way in establishing relationships, and that's exactly what you are doing: building relationships!

Don't Be Afraid to Reach Out Directly

Most forms of social media have a direct messaging feature. This will allow you the opportunity to engage with those you have connected with on a deeper level. As you casually interact with your PLN online, you will naturally begin to establish relationships that become more significant over time. When this happens and you feel the right level of comfort with a particular connection, it may be okay to reach out via direct messaging. This could be to extend a conversation by taking it from public to private, to do a personal check-in with someone, to simply drop in to say hello, or to thank someone for something wonderful they shared.

Sending direct messages to those within your circle will allow you to build trusting relationships and to engage on a more personal level with your PLN. The one-on-one conversations you engage in using direct messaging will also help to catapult your learning because the deep communication we have with others works to broaden our understanding about the topics that matter to us.

Your PLN Should Be an Intentionally Designed Village, Too

Since many of us are actively involved in doing the work to become unbiased, antiracist educators, our PLN should include the perspectives of a diverse array of individuals. When engaging with your online PLN, be sure to find and follow the voices of experts in the fields of social justice, racism, and equity, as well as experts who can help you meet the needs of your Black and Brown students, your LGBTQ community, Native and Indigenous people, Asian Americans and Pacific Islanders, and any other marginalized populations you might serve in your classroom. Our connections need to transcend the boundaries that limit, exclude, or silence voices that have been left unheard. Intentionally designing our PLN means we are taking steps toward developing awareness, empathy, tolerance, and respect for every student who enters our classrooms. Our PLN should be representative of the students we serve, or could serve, as we carry out our work as educators.

JOINING TWITTER CHATS

Chats are one of the best features for learning on Twitter. By joining these online discussion forums, you will gain access to some of the greatest minds in education. While participating, you will interact with and learn from people everywhere who are experts in all facets of education. Teachers, administrators, thought leaders, coaches, and more participate in Twitter chats, in which moderators pose groups of questions during a designated time period to be answered by participants.

Participation is easy, and you can join by simply searching for the hashtag of the chat you are looking for. Once prompted, introduce yourself, then answer each question posed in the format required by the moderator. Be sure to include the hashtag. If you do not, your answer will not show up in the chat feed and others can't respond to you. Once you answer a question, your response will appear along with everyone else's in the chat feed. You won't believe how quickly you'll get used to participating in these fast-paced online discussions. The rest is easy: just grab yourself a beverage and snack, find a comfy spot, and get chatting! You'll be amazed at what you will learn and feel excitement about the fabulous connections you'll make with passionate educators just like yourself.

Twitter chats provide the opportunity to learn about many education topics based on the area of interest you choose: ed tech, whole child education, social-emotional learning, antiracism education, and school leadership, just to name a few. Your favorite influencers and education experts usually have lists of their favorite chats or chats they moderate listed in their profiles. This is a great way to find new chats. Of course, you could always tweet out asking for information about the best edchats, but beware, you'll be blown away by the responses you get!

BE PREPARED FOR MAGIC TO HAPPEN

As you continue your learning journey through your chosen social media platform(s), you will likely discover many more amazing things you can do to develop yourself as an educator. Not only will you grow yourself and your PLN, but you will also gain access to many unique opportunities to engage with educators around the world. Through the self-development process, you will begin to feel more confident about sharing your own voice. You might find yourself with invites to guest moderate Twitter chats, do Instagram takeovers, appear on podcasts, guest write on other people's blogs, contribute to articles and website content, and so much more.

For business owners and entrepreneurs, social media is a powerful marketing tool. For teachers, however, it becomes a think tank of sorts, filled with educators set upon working together to change the face of education. Whatever your preferred way of connecting, teachers find comfort in knowing they are not alone in their fight to educate every student by creating inclusive and authentic learning experiences that meet the needs of every child. By engaging with other teachers through social media, we are taking deliberate steps to grow ourselves by learning with and from our peers.

When they belong to a PLN, new teachers lose their feelings of isolation and gain much-needed confidence. Veteran teachers experience a sense of camaraderie as they are inspired by working with others to reimagine education. In PLNs, teachers lift each other up. They encourage, inspire, praise, and respect one another. Where educator PLNs gather, magic happens—magic that drives purpose, fuels passions, and changes the world.

SHARE YOUR BRILLIANCE WITH THE WORLD

Teaching may well be considered an art to some, but you have worked hard to hone your skills and increase your knowledge, and because of that, you have the ability to create learning masterpieces in your classroom every day. You know how to engage students and plan dynamic lessons that are inclusive, differentiated, and of course, steeped in antiracism. You are an accomplished educator (and you have the evaluations to prove it!), and you have a ride-or-die PLN committed to doing whatever it takes to make school a better place for kids. You have the mindset of a professional. You know your purpose. It's time to take your show on the road.

Once you have made the decision to aim for greatness in the classroom, you will see all sorts of transformations begin to take place in your professional life. You will become more confident because you have taken great strides to master your craft. Others will seek your advice and input on how to tackle issues in their classrooms. Your peers will want to observe you at work with students, and they will want your feedback on their teaching practice. You will support these folks as they come to you with their questions and inquiries, because you are an educator and that's what educators do: we help one another.

And when you begin broadening your PLN by connecting with other education professionals, both online and in person, you will find yourself with some extraordinary opportunities to engage with the education world. By attending conferences, online webinars, and Zoom meetups; moderating and participating in Twitter chats; hosting online watch parties; doing radio show drop-ins, podcast recordings, and Facebook livestreams; and engaging in so many more amazing experiences, I have been able to grow my PLN to include phenomenal educators from almost every corner of the globe—and so can you!

Conferences. Whether it's in person or virtual, I bet you get an invitation in your email inbox at least once a week to attend a local, national, or regional conference. Take a closer look, because somewhere in that jumbled mix of information, you will see a link that says, "Call for Presenters." Remember that rock-star lesson you gave last week or last month? Go ahead and submit a proposal to present that to conference attendees. You'll have a follow-up email before you know it letting you know you've been selected to host your own session or workshop.

Podcasts. Podcasts are everywhere and cover every topic imaginable, inside of education and out. When you become an active part of a PLN, chances are someone in it is a podcaster, and you will soon be invited to take a seat at the mic. Don't shy away from the opportunity. People are eager to hear your story. And if you don't feel like waiting for an invite, then start your own podcast! There are plenty of free resources and podcasting platforms available to help you get off the ground.

Blogging. Creating your own teaching blog is as easy as 1-2-3. There are a wide variety of platforms that make blogging easy.

WordPress, Wix, or Squarespace will have you up and running in no time. Use your blog as a place to reflect on your practice, to tell the world about new resources you have discovered, or to share lessons you have learned in your work as a teacher so that others can grow through your stories. Be on the lookout for opportunities to guest blog, too. Organizations and individuals are always looking for new voices to share what's working in their classrooms and schools.

Coaching and mentoring. You don't have to have a formal title as instructional coach or mentor to be able to help your peers. There may be resident educators or preservice teachers assigned to your classroom or your building who are in need of just the kind of experience you have. You can provide support with developing lesson plans and assignments and activities related to coursework, or simply share some insight on the things about which they are curious.

Writing articles. Educational journals, online magazines, and websites like Medium.com, Edutopia.org, and ASCD.org are continually on the hunt for educators who are eager to share their classroom stories. Write alone or with a peer. This is another excellent way to grow your PLN.

Authoring your own book. Yes. You absolutely can write a book. It takes time, energy, focus, and commitment. But if you have a story to tell, tell it. Someone out there is just waiting for you to turn your wisdom into words so they can learn from you.

This list of professional opportunities is far from comprehensive. There is always a need for educators who are willing to share their brilliance: district in-service days, state and local associations, university events, local or national TED Talks, local educational service centers, even international organizations. The opportunities are endless; you just have to go find them!

While you are at work helping to change the face of education, don't forget to keep your résumé up to date. You never know when you might need it. Add sections for "Professional Presentations" and

"Publications," and include any other activities you have been involved in that served to advance the education of others. That is real work. Valuable work. Others may need to see that someday. And while you are at it, don't forget to curate your online experiences. Create a digital portfolio in Wakelet or on Google Sites that offers a glimpse at how you are leaving your mark on the world.

If your goal is to become the best teacher you can possibly be, then take steps to find others who are on the journey toward greatness and continue toward your destination together. Complainers and Negative Nellies are everywhere, but you want to spend your time around people who are laser-focused on being the best versions of themselves. Robert John Meehan said, "A key to growing as an educator is to keep company mainly with educators who uplift you, whose presence inspires you and whose dedication drives you."[1] Keep that kind of company, for sure, but also strive to *be* that kind of company.

---

1   Robert J. Meehan, *Teacher's Journey: The Road Less Traveled* (Mustang, OK: Tate Pub & Enterprises, 2011).

SAIL ON

✕ If you haven't already, join Twitter, Instagram, Facebook, or another social media site. After you have set up your profile, go find and follow your favorite education leaders, authors, and colleagues. Once you do, be courageous and share something on your timeline that you think will help others.

✕ If you already have a social media account but haven't been that active, reintroduce yourself to the world. On Twitter, go find an upcoming chat and drop in for some conversation. Don't forget to invite your PLC to also become part of your online PLN. Share what you've learned and who you've met in your next PLC meeting.

✕ Start that blog you've been thinking about, or dust yours off if you haven't posted in a while. Write about a recent lesson or activity that went well, or share a recent success you have had in your classroom. Share your post on social media. Don't forget to tag me, @DHarrisEdS, and others in your PLN so we can all learn from your expertise!

✕ Make sure your PLN is diverse. Think about the students you serve and your goal of becoming an antiracist educator. Who are the folks who can support you in doing so? Connect with experts like Dena Simmons, Ken Shelton, Rosa Perez-Isiah, and others who can help you become more confident as you carry out this work. Also consider who in your building may be willing to go on the journey to becoming an antiracist educator with you. Explore and learn together. Engage one another in conversation surrounding antiracism. Make plans to be there for one another when setbacks occur, and push each other to keep pressing forward.

EIGHT

Your Best Evaluation Yet

If we create a culture where every teacher believes they need to improve, not because they are not good enough but because they can be even better, there is no limit to what we can achieve.

—DYLAN WILIAM

Spoiler Alert: The decision to put PIRATE planning at the heart of your practice has the potential to move you from an average educator to an accomplished one in no time at all. Seriously. By committing to intentional, well in advance of schedule, engaging, antiracist, student-centered planning, you gain the power to drastically transform how your administrator evaluates your practice and how your students experience learning in your classroom. No ifs. No ands. No buts. PIRATE planning puts *your* professional success in *your* hands.

∽

I don't know about you, but I am always up for a good challenge. I have the kind of brain that responds to phrases like "You can't" with "Watch me." So when evaluation season arrives, I love challenging myself to be better than the time before. As a PIRATE planner, that becomes an easy task because every component of the evaluation rubric is already at work in your classroom and in your professional life on the daily.

What's also terrific about the evaluation process is that it offers us the chance to dive deep into self-reflective thinking about how our practice impacts the students we serve, and for as much as we want to perform well on our evaluations, our main priority and focus should always be to spotlight the learning that occurs as a result of our practice. While evaluations are a process as much as anything else, they provide us with a unique opportunity to shine a light on the hard work we have been doing to make learning amazing for everyone involved. While your administrator may be thoroughly impressed at the magic they witness, kids won't know the difference because you teach and plan the PIRATE way whether it's evaluation season or not. Learning in your class is always transformational!

GAME ON

I like to think of evaluation day as game day. Your administrator shows up to see an awesome performance, and you won't let them down because you've been putting in the work and practicing your best strategies all year long, so it's inevitable you're going to score big! But we can't get too caught up in focusing on the score alone. Yes, a good score means a win for sure, but in education, we work in a field where if you are savvy enough, you could strategize a good enough performance to get a win; unfortunately, that game-day performance would look very different from what your administrator might see if they popped in any other day, and we don't want that. Our kids don't want that. How we show up and show out on game day should be what our kiddos see us doing every day.

In a motivational speech given to North Carolina State University's Wolfpack football team, Dr. Eric Thomas spoke frankly to a group of players who seemed to be enjoying the limelight associated with their budding football careers. During his recorded speech, Dr. Thomas said something that really resonated with me. In his matter-of-fact tone, he said to the players, "Some of you just want to score. You don't like the process. You're not in love with the process. You have to love the process as much as you love the prize."[1]

Upon hearing his words, I realized Thomas's advice to those players applies to any human being striving to reach greatness: football players, business professionals, educators, anyone. It's true that a good majority of folks want to excel at what they do and enjoy success, even be able to bask in it, perhaps. But if we don't love the work it takes to reach the success we want so badly, well, success isn't likely to happen in the first place. Like Thomas encouraged those football players to learn to enjoy their practice and hard work, educators also need to learn to love the process of refinement and practicing new strategies so that we can reach next-level greatness, too. Then, when game day rolls around, the performance you deliver via the evaluation process will offer undeniable proof that you "love the process as much as you love the prize," and game day could be literally any day your administrator decides to walk into your room. With the kind of mindset Thomas encourages us to embrace, every day in your classroom is preparation for game day, not *just* the days or weeks before your evaluation, and PIRATE planning is the key that will help you deliver your best evaluation yet!

PIRATE PLANNING GIVES WAY TO ACCOMPLISHED TEACHING

When you plan like a PIRATE, the evaluation cycle is a walk in the park. You have incorporated real-world, student-centered, standards-based, differentiated learning into everything you do in your classroom. You're ready to show off your skills!

---

1   Eric Thomas, "ET Speaks to Wolfpack Football," NCStatePackFootball, YouTube, 5:35, https://www.youtube.com/watch?v=el5KqBGd01M.

In most cases, you should know well in advance of your evaluation session when your administrator will be coming in to observe you. At the moment you know, you should already have your planning wheels in motion as you begin to design the learning you want for your administrator to evaluate, and more importantly for your students to experience—that's who this whole process is about, after all. Here's a key point that may help you as you begin planning for your evaluation: your administrator is not the enemy. They are not there to beat you up with harsh criticisms about all you did wrong. Their role is to work with you to ensure that you are providing students with a high-quality education that meets their needs. The evaluation process gives them the information they need to be able to do that. But have no fear: you are going to knock their socks off because you are a PIRATE planner and you have been working toward your prize long before they ever walked into your classroom to watch you create magic.

When introducing a rubric to my students, I always tell them to begin planning their performance by looking at the column indicating the highest level of performance and telling themselves, "This is where I want to be." I say this to remind my students—and you as well—that while they aren't just after a perfect score, by using this standard of measurement they can easily demonstrate that they have mastered their craft at the highest level possible. Setting high expectations should not be something we only ask our students to do. We should do this ourselves. To begin your preplanning, pull out your state or district's evaluation rubric and refamiliarize yourself with what is in the most accomplished rating column. Start there before you begin inputting anything into any kind of evaluation platform database or required documentation instrument.

On the rubric, you are going to find a number of standards-based categories that look something like the ones below. Let's take a minute and break down how PIRATE planning is embedded into every facet of our evaluation process.

Knowledge of Your Students

Because you are a PIRATE planner, you have taken action to create a classroom culture built on strong relationships and a sense of belonging. You know about your students as learners because you have been observing them as such all year long, providing them feedback, incorporating their individual learning styles, and engaging them in student-centered activities each day. You have analyzed oodles of data that tells you what your students can or cannot do, both in the context of your curriculum and out of it. Through the establishment of rigorous, tiered learning targets, you have set high expectations for every student. You are focused on becoming an antiracist educator, and because of that, you have learned much about your students as individuals and their values and beliefs and you have developed a mutual respect for one another. Their identification status and intervention requirements are probably just a mouse click away. You know your students, and you know them well.

Command of Your Content

For most educators, to say that you know your content would be an understatement. We chose our content area for a reason, and most of the time, that involves having a deep passion for the subject matter. However, if you are novice educator or a veteran looking to develop yourself, and you are taking steps to become a PIRATE planner, then you are making a habit of looking at assessment data regularly. That data will point you to specific areas in the content where you may need to refine your own knowledge and skills to be able to help students show growth. Ask yourself where the data says you need to focus your attention for students, and study that content if you are struggling there yourself. Provide the research and analysis you conduct as part of your evidentiary documentation to show you are working to gain a command of your content. Remember, showing you are growing is equally as acceptable as showing mastery. Don't beat yourself up if you have work to do. We all have work to do.

Because you have also made the commitment to CHARTing a course to a better world as you build out learning within the context of your curriculum, you are able to connect learning to real-life experiences. And by launching learning with Wonderings to get students excited about learning, you will easily be able to show how what students learn ties directly to the world outside your classroom. You can make these connections yourself in your evaluation documentation so that your administrator can see, but a more impactful piece of evidence will be exemplars of your students' own work that show the same thing. These are game changers in the evaluation process and can move you from skilled to accomplished in no time.

Use of Assessment

Assessment is the core of everything we do as PIRATE teachers and planners. We have to know where our students are in the curriculum and what they are able to do, and we get that information from assessment data. We have to be able to confidently state where we want our students to be at the end of a learning segment, and we use assessment data to establish that. We ask our students to show mastery of the concepts and skills we engage them in exploring—yep, you guessed it: assessment data. You are creating, administering, and evaluating assessments every single day. You use diagnostic, benchmark, and formative assessments to discover valuable, informative data about your students in every step of your practice. You have used that data to provide differentiated learning targets that further serve to show you know your students, inside and out. And not only that, but as part of the Essential Eight planning framework, you have already built the delivery of high-quality, meaningful feedback into your practice. In fact, students have come to expect it. You have evidence of the time you have built into your framework as well as students' own peer feedback and self-reflections to show application of that feedback. And while we're talking about students, don't forget that personal goal setting you did with them. That applies here, too. When talking about assessments, include how students are making progress toward their own personal goals, because after all, the evaluation is more about students than it is about you.

Delivery of Instruction

You are a PIRATE teacher and a PIRATE planner. Your instruction is life changing for kids, and you need to be proud of that. Every school or district requires that teachers align their instructional practice with some set of local or regional standards. Big deal. You can do that with your eyes closed. Once you have identified in your content area what students need to be able to do to show growth, go find that in the standards and use the language in crafting your learning targets. This is routine—or at least it should be. How you ensure those standards remain at the forefront of your practice, however, relies on how well you have planned out the coordinating learning experiences.

Long before delivering any instruction, PIRATE planners have taken steps to craft tailored learning targets that students will use to identify their own academic goals, and that you will use to plan the learning experiences that depend upon your guidance as the teacher. In doing so, you will have made learning relevant to students' lives; you will have designed authentic, student-led activities that allow students independence in showing mastery of their learning. Your well-planned Essential Eight framework includes concept-based learning, critical thinking and inquiry, constructed response, purposeful use of technology, and more, all of which will show your administrator that you know how to use data, how to tap into student interests and support students throughout learning. The Essential Eight framework is *the* model for the "accomplished" delivery of instruction. Use it!

The Learning Environment

First and foremost, you have been hard at work deepening your own awareness as you grow to become an antiracist educator. The steps you take in this area will open your eyes to your own privilege and the hidden biases you may not have even known you possessed. You have begun to see your students as distinctly different from one another, as you should. They *are* different, and that may mean they need different supports—supports that aren't always equal, but that *are* equitable. Be prepared to talk with your administrator about this in your pre- and postevaluation conferences. Let them know your goals in seeking to become actively antiracist and what that means for you and for your students.

Show your administrator how you are working to ensure your classroom is safe for every student. Share with them what steps you have taken to make your classroom fully inclusive and a place where belonging is the core. Explain that as the chief engagement officer of your classroom, you have taken every step possible to remove barriers between your students and learning. You have a well-designed structure within your online learning platform that allows every student access to the resources and materials they need to be able to perform successfully every day. Students know where to go for information and can advocate for themselves, and you have gone to great measures to plan learning experiences that keep kids engaged from bell to bell. Your learning environment is on fire, and kids are running in ready to learn. Your administrator will see that as soon as students begin walking into your room on evaluation day.

Collaboration and Communication

It's clear that many of us want to be part of something bigger. If this is you, then your PLC and your PLN will become the backbone of your success. They'll keep you focused and grounded, and continuously challenge you to be the best version of yourself by engaging you in thoughtful dialogue and learning surrounding your practice. You'll learn from them, with them, and through them. Together, you'll reimagine the ways in which you bring educational experiences to kids. During your preconference, talk with your administrator about how you are networking and collaborating with others. Tell them what your PLC is working on together and let them know how you have grown through interactions with your PLN. You are doing amazing things together—share that!

When you built your platform for learning, whether in Google Classroom, Microsoft Teams, or another school-based learning management system, you gave yourself the ability to hand parents and caregivers the keys to your classroom. As our partners in helping students show growth, we also need to give parents and caregivers the ability to monitor students' progress toward the goals we set for them. By adding parents to your email distribution list, Remind app groups, or online classroom or by sharing your class website with them, you are engaging them in constant communication about what is happening in the classroom and where their student is in the grand scheme of things. You've crafted a syllabus that serves as a one-stop shop for information on how to contact you, as well as classroom codes to apps and programs that may be helpful to them as parents. Your level of communication with parents is above and beyond. Share this with your administrator by printing out or downloading emails and other classroom communications as evidence of your accomplishments.

Professionalism

Our professionalism is the life breath of our practice. The steps we take to become better educators for kids can make all the difference in their lives and ours. By default, our profession requires that we continue our education in order to maintain our legal right to practice, so we are constantly in search of ways to improve our performance and expand our knowledge base surrounding our effectiveness as educators. During your preconference, share with your administrator what books you are reading, or if you are taking coursework or seeking to expand your licensure. Have you attended webinars, conferences, or any other collaborative learning experiences online? Tell them what you learned and how you are applying it in your classroom. Be sure to tell your administrator about your commitment to becoming a

PIRATE planner and all that comes along with that title. Your decision to do so means you are transforming your teaching practice such that it will have a profound impact on students and your role as a change agent. State your aim to continuously focus on greatness in all you do for kids. Tell them that.

You are a PIRATE planner. You know what you are doing in your classroom. Every single action, every strategy, every model of student work, and every plan you have made and executed is evidence of your expertise. So if your goal is to be called an "accomplished" educator, you have zero excuses. Be one.

EVERY SINGLE ACTION, EVERY STRATEGY, EVERY MODEL OF STUDENT WORK, AND EVERY PLAN YOU HAVE MADE AND EXECUTED IS EVIDENCE OF YOUR EXPERTISE.

PLAN THE PERFORMANCE EVERYONE EXPECTS TO SEE

Now that you know you have what it takes to win big on game day (and every other day!), it's time to choose your class and content for observation so that you can begin preparation to reach the performance metric you deserve. I recognize that we may not all have the advantage of preselecting our class period (time or space), but we do have the power to control what we teach and how we teach it. If you are fully immersed in PIRATE planning, you may have already constructed plans for learning that could be used as the focus of your observation. If your observation is so far out that you haven't fully planned that learning yet, then it's never too early to get started.

Using PIRATE planning methods to build out your learning will help you to put together the step-by-step of what your administrator will see you doing on observation day. Orchestrating the learning you want your administrator to observe involves three simple actions.

1. Wakelet is a fabulous curation tool and works amazingly for organizing performance evaluations. I use it to sort my evidence of mastery for each of the professional teaching standards set forth by the evaluation instrument. I create a new collection for each evaluation, and as a result, I have a running portfolio of evaluation material if I ever need to refer back to it.

2. I also prepare some sort of data analysis worksheet using Excel or Google Sheets that shows student performance levels and that establishes my rationale for the data-driven, high-quality instruction I have prepared.

3. Next, I use the Essential Eight framework to build out my assessment and learning activities for the segment I will be presenting. You can find a copy of the framework template online at www.educationundone.com on the "Plan Like a PIRATE" tab.

Just like when we plan learning for our students, as we prepare for the evaluation process, we should also begin with our desired outcomes in mind. This is where we get to dig deep into our students' performance assessment data (and this won't just be test data) to determine the focal point for instruction based on students' needs. Use your data analysis worksheet to organize the data you selected to determine students' learning needs. Once you have analyzed the data, summarize your analysis, explain your grouping strategy, and share your tailored learning targets. Add this document to your Wakelet collection as it is the justification for your decision to teach this particular lesson and touches on several standards for measurement in the evaluation rubric.

The Essential Eight planning framework will be your guide for the design and delivery of high-quality instruction on observation day. Use the learning targets and your choice of differentiated, student-centered formative assessments to craft the learning experience your students need. Include the essential practices from the framework in every facet of your teaching. Your unit will be concept based, you will include academic and domain-specific language, and your students will use technology that serves to advance their growth rather than fill a hole. You will be asking your students deep questions that stir in them a thirst for information, and you will observe and encourage them as they write out those thoughts and share them with others, building relationships as they do. You will provide your students with meaningful feedback, and they will reward themselves with a commitment to engagement from bell to bell. This is the Essential Eight in action. It is the blueprint for great teaching and the evidence for rock-solid PIRATE planning.

PREPARING FOR THE PRECONFERENCE

To get ready for your preconference, gather all the evidence you will present to your administrator together in one place. In the past, I have used plain manila folders, one for me and one for my administrator, in which I placed printed copies of everything; however, I no longer do that. Since Wakelet has become my go-to spot for organizing everything I need for my observation, I add PDF copies of my preconference documentation as well as my lesson plans and links to evidence and resources I reference in my planning documents. I also make sure my administrator has been added to the Google Classroom for the group of students they will be observing, and I add that link to the Wakelet space, too. If your administrator is open to viewing your materials digitally, you can share your Wakelet with them. Every single thing they need is there, and all you have to do is provide one single link that gives them access to all your evaluation materials. No duplicate copies, nothing. All they get from you is a digital experience filled with every shred of evidence they need. Another bonus your digital collection offers is that if your administrator is still in need of evidence from you in crucial areas after your postconference, you can go ahead and let them know you'll add that missing information into the Wakelet for their review. They will love the ease of access, along with the fact that they won't be bombarded with tons and tons of paperwork!

Reflect on your preparation process and what you want your performance to look like in advance of your preconference. Don't show up cold. Anticipate what your administrator is going to ask you, and be ready to answer with evidence. On preconference day, walk your administrator through exactly what they are going to see. Don't make them have to look for a single thing when they arrive in your classroom on game day. You told them what they were going to see; now show them!

IT'S GAME DAY—TIME TO DO YOU

Be confident on evaluation day because you have prepared an amazing learning experience built on every principle of PIRATE planning, and that means your administrator is about to be wowed. For your students, however, this will just be another day in the classroom.

You may find that your administrator arrives before students, or sometimes they will arrive after instruction has already begun. This is of no consequence. You can fill in any gaps during your postconference. And the fact that another adult has arrived in the room shouldn't mean much to students if you have been hard at work creating an intentionally designed village already. New faces won't be a surprise, and having an administrator in the room just gives students a chance to show off their skills as learners, too. It's up to you whether or not you advise students ahead of time that an administrator is coming to evaluate you. I do not. I never have, simply because I don't want students to feel like they are the ones having to perform. Students are going to be up to the same things they have been day after day in your classroom, so telling them ahead of time shouldn't matter.

Key point to remember: While the learning that is taking place in your classroom is all about your students, the ability to execute great teaching is all about you. This is the *why* behind the observation process. You certainly don't want students feeling like they are the players in the game. They are the pieces that you guide and move through learning so you can declare your victory as an excellent educator. As long as you know the deal, that's all that matters.

Before you carry out your observation lesson, you have to know ahead of time to anticipate setbacks, before, during, and after your evaluation. Maybe you woke up not feeling well or have some emotional or personal struggles that are impacting your focus. Perhaps you planned some intentional grouping and several students are absent, requiring you to adjust groups on the fly. Or maybe a new student shows up and you have zero information about them and have to figure out in a few short seconds how to get them introduced to the class and then engaged in what you hope is a developmentally appropriate group. You have to think clearly before your evaluation about what kinds of things can happen, so that if they do, you will be prepared. I know it's unrealistic to know everything that might happen, but if we have thoroughly planned and thought about what we want observation day to look, feel, and sound like, we have also taken steps in that planning to consider the unforeseen. Half of winning any battle is knowing that the unexpected is your primary enemy. So, expect the unexpected!

You've put in the work ahead of time, so during the observation, you should know when and where you are falling short. When something doesn't feel right in the process of your actual teaching, make a mental note and go back later and jot that down as a point to explore when you engage in self-reflection and in your postconference afterward. Remember, you've done all the right planning. You know what you are doing. You are in control, and you are going to be great!

THE POSTCONFERENCE WRAP-UP

Your postconference should be your time to celebrate! Be excited for feedback from your administrator. Their job is to support you in your growth. Listen to their concerns, and be open to receiving their support. As I've stated before, we all have work to do, and this is just one single evaluation of your performance. We will always have another chance to do better. On every evaluation day, be proud of the fact that you continually embrace the process of growth and because of that you (and your students) are always winners! You are a PIRATE planner, and you own your success.

NaViGaTiNG Your JouRNey to AnTiRacist EduCaToR

As you set about the work of becoming an antiracist educator with the mindset that you are responsible for your own journey to awareness and growth, you will seek the input and support of others. You will read about, research, inquire, and reflect on the history and perspectives necessary to bring you toward understanding as it pertains to the lived experiences of the marginalized and historically oppressed people around you. You will reflect on all you have learned and allow it to transform your thinking about how society views and treats people of color, ethnic minorities, and the other underrepresented groups that may enter into your classroom or your life daily.

In your work, you will come to realize that there are things you were unaware of about yourself as a human being and as an educator that may have affected your ability to see yourself or your attitudes as racist. These discoveries may be uncomfortable, even painful at times, but to be able to implement antiracist teaching practices in your classroom, you will need to arrive at this work with an attitude of courage and empathy if you expect to grow.

On your journey, you will also come to see that you are not alone, that we all have work to do in becoming actively antiracist. When you do decide to embark on this journey, when you finally realize that it is your responsibility and your obligation to use your voice to help amplify the silenced voices of others, you will see a shift in yourself, in the way in which you see and value others.

BE GREAT BEING YOU

While you probably spent hours filling out your preconference forms and gathering evidence, your observation is supposed to represent you being your everyday version of great in the classroom, just you being your authentic self among the children you love and care for. The things you will do in your classroom will be the same things you would do on any other day, or at least they should be. After all, why would you do anything less for your kids? Would you want them asking themselves or one another after observation day, "Geez, why doesn't she teach like that all the time?" Otherwise, you might be left asking yourself, *Do I really deserve that rating I so badly wanted?* When you are in love with the process, you will feel good knowing that what you earned, you deserve.

You are a dynamic force in the classroom. As a PIRATE teacher, your passion and enthusiasm bring an energy to learning unlike any other. When you plan like a PIRATE, the evidence will be clear that you have spent time, well in advance, to prepare extraordinary lear-ing journeys for every student. Your commitment to the PIRATE way means you won't just become a good teacher, you'll be a great one!

SAIL ON

✘ Pull out your most recent evaluation and reflect on your performance. Identify those areas in which you performed lowest. Make that an area of focus in your practice between now and your next evaluation cycle. Share your goals with your administrator, and the next time they are free, invite them to walk through and provide input based on what they observe is happening in your classroom.

✘ Consider when you will be evaluated next. Where in your curriculum will you be? What will students have studied by that time? Evaluate the relationships and classroom culture you have established already. Which class, what data, and what content might you include as part of the evaluation process? Why?

✘ Begin game-day preplanning right now by considering what area of growth you feel you need to focus on most. Once you have come to a decision about the plan for learning you will implement during the upcoming evaluation, begin assembling your evidence and data to support the high-quality instruction you will demonstrate to your observing administrator.

✘ Craft your mission and vision for becoming an antiracist educator. Even if your administrator doesn't ask during your evaluation, be courageous in sharing your goals with them. Share what you've learned, and be prepared to provide them with examples of the work your students have done in becoming actively antiracist themselves. Let your administrator know this is important work for you, but it is more important for students as you help them navigate the complexities of the world around them through the content you teach.

The Impact of Our Greatness

Remember Julie, my PIRATE art teacher? She impacted my life in so many ways, but I know mine wasn't the only one. She steered my life in a different direction because of the teacher she was. Julie taught her students about the important things that mattered in life: how to love others, how to seek understanding, to advocate for ourselves and other people. She inspired in us an unending sense of curiosity, and more important than anything, she showed us the power of hope. Julie engaged us in every way through the learning she so carefully crafted for each one of us.

I recall all of this with such clarity. In 1988, I didn't have a single plan to become a teacher, but now that I am one, I am able to see how amazing Julie was. She was my hero then, and she is an even bigger hero to me now that I *am* an educator. She is everything I try to be for my students every single day.

Our own passion and energy has the potential to fill our students up and leave them feeling as if they can accomplish anything. I will never in my life forget how Julie made me feel. When they enter into our classrooms, we should want the very same for our students. This takes focus, dedication, love, and a commitment to doing whatever it takes to *be great* throughout our careers as educators.

EDUCATION UNDONE

In 2017, I had the pleasure of attending an Ohio Leadership Advisory Council conference at The Ohio State University where Cathy Lassiter, author of *Everyday Courage for School Leaders*, gave an amazing keynote speech. In her presentation, Lassiter spoke to her audience about the importance of never feeling as if you have "arrived" in education, that you have come to some spot in your career where you simply can't get any better. That was an eye-opening statement to me. Not because I felt like it pertained to me; on the contrary, I know I will *always* be a work in progress, but my curiosity was piqued and I sat up to listen because, by all means, I never wanted to feel that way about myself.

That day, I resolved that greatness would be something I would continually seek to achieve. You see, I agree with Lassiter. I believe no matter how great a teacher we might become or how successful we envision ourselves to be, we will always have work to do in improving ourselves as educators. Because we are humans, teachers, individuals who care about ourselves and our students, our personal journey of growth will never be complete. We can never stop learning because we can't ever afford to stop growing. We have to accept that to be great means our education will forever be undone.

In his book *Culturize*, Jimmy Casas said, "Great leaders can inspire average teachers back to greatness," and I believe the same is true for educators. Great educators can inspire greatness in both their students *and* their colleagues. When we do better, when we are better educators, our students are better, our professional cohort is better, and our school becomes better, too. Much rests on our greatness in the classroom. We should always work hard to become the best versions of ourselves possible.

UNDOING TO REIMAGINE

If you will, please grab a notebook or your journal and open it to a new page, or open a new note or document on your electronic device.

Across the top, title your page "Undo List."

I know you're thinking, *Wait, what is she asking me to do?*

Well, typically, when we find ourselves with many tasks to accomplish, we create ourselves a to-do list, right? What I'm asking you instead is to make the commitment from this point forward to remain equally as focused on what you need to *un*do as much as you need *to* do in order to make learning and school better for kids. Now that you are a PIRATE teacher *and* a PIRATE planner and possess all the insights of what great teaching looks, feels, and sounds like, you have the ability to look past conventional ways of "doing" education and instead can work to *undo* education, transforming it into something better, something entirely new. We often hear this packaged as "reimagining education."

What you put on your list will be up to you. But I do know this list could be as endless as our to-do lists, and I also know that this undo list has the potential to affect change far more than our to-do lists ever could.

Just considering some challenges we have faced thus far in the twenty-first century, I'd say there's already plenty for us to undo. Perhaps we can work toward undoing things like

- Student Labeling that Influences Expectations
- Gender Gaps in Educational Achievement
- Overuse of Standardized Testing
- Implementing Programs in Place of People
- Educational Inequities that Inhibit Learning
- The School-to-Prison Pipeline
- Ignoring Social-Emotional Learning
- Lack of Diversity in Teaching Staff

There are literally hundreds of things we could add to these undo lists that are key to transforming schools and kids' lives. Our combined collection of undo lists grants us the ability to reimagine learning as we seek to create new experiences that will grow engaged, inspired, lifelong learners. We have tremendous power to shape the lives of our students who will, in turn, shape the future. Educators must fully embrace a "by any means necessary" attitude when it comes to meeting the needs of our kids, including having the courage to tackle tough issues that affect our students even when others will not.

> ## EDUCATORS MUST FULLY EMBRACE A "BY ANY MEANS NECESSARY" ATTITUDE WHEN IT COMES TO MEETING THE NEEDS OF OUR KIDS.

Infinitely Reimagining Education

We have yet to fully understand the work that lies ahead of us in this field. Our profession changes at lightning pace, and to switch gears and adjust our teaching to meet the demands of the system and the needs of our students simultaneously on a dime is no easy task. But we do it, and we do it without hesitation. What educators and administrators faced in 2020 alone, with the arrival of the COVID-19 pandemic, was unprecedented. In a few short weeks, the face of school was transformed to provide students with access to education delivered straight to their living rooms, bedrooms, and kitchens, while moms, dads, aunties, uncles, grandmas, and grandpas worked beside them navigating the unfamiliar waters of being at-home workers and teacher aides at the same time. But this isn't the only challenge we've faced as educators. We have had to help students come to understand the impacts of systemic racism and the social injustices that have plagued our society, yet been ignored, for countless decades. Our work in recent years has been some of the hardest we have ever done. Every day, teachers show up in schools where the threat of gun violence is real. We take to the streets of our communities and the halls of our schools and political institutions to fight against the inequities that harm our kids and for educational reform. We spend our own time and money to make sure no child goes without whatever they need to feel safe and loved while in our care. Teachers do whatever necessary to be there for kids. We knew what we signed up for when we choose the title "teacher." It's who we are.

Since the beginning of my teaching career, so much has changed: standards, federal regulations, mandates, policy, local to federal education leadership, just to name a few. New trends emerge by the minute, technology by the second, it seems. I can only imagine what education will be like ten years from now. So it isn't enough to focus on our own improvement. We must focus on the ways in which we have to undo and reimagine education for every child. John Dewey said, "If we teach today as we taught yesterday, we rob our children of tomorrow," and he was exactly right. We cannot afford to embrace a "we've always done it this way" mindset. It's bad for us, and it's worse for our kids.

OUR WHY

Usually, it's at the beginning of any new journey that we find ourselves discussing our *why*, the reason we do what we do. But we really didn't need to do that here. We are teachers; we know our why, and it's not a *what*, it's a *who*. And when we say we know our students, we mean we *know* them. We know their needs. We know their struggles. We know that there is potential in every one of them to be something great, even if they don't know that yet themselves.

It was Rita Pierson, one of the most influential educators of all time, who taught us that our primary responsibility as educators is to be champions for our students. In the parting words of her world-renowned TED Talk, Pierson left her audience with this: "Is this job tough? You betcha. Oh God, you betcha. But it is not impossible. We can do this. We're educators. We're born to make a difference."

In the seven and a half minutes I spent listening to Pierson's speech for the very first time, my mind was made up. I wasn't going to be an average teacher—ever. We have the most amazing job in the world, and young people are depending on us to show up for them day in and day out. We may be the only champion some of our students ever have. I vowed never to take that responsibility lightly.

Since then, I bet I have listened to Pierson's speech a hundred times. She put into words what we should all seek to be every day, in every way. Greatness in the classroom became my goal. My kids, my why.

So I leave you with this, just a few of the words that gave me the momentum to write this very book, the reason I do what I do . . .

> To Mrs. Harris,
>
> I want to say thank you. Thank you for being the smart, kind human being all of your students know you to be. Thank you for going above and beyond your everyday duties to make sure your students succeed in life. Thank you for pushing everyone to be their best selves.
>
> You are the kind of person whose warmth and positivity radiates like the sun. Thank you for supporting and encouraging me. I learned a lot more than just English because of your willingness to share knowledge. I am a better person, and I will always be grateful for you. The impact you made on me is everlasting, and I know each of your students is equally as lucky to call you their teacher.
>
> And thank you most of all for being the inspirational and amazing human being that you so effortlessly are each and every day.

Now, go, my friends. Begin your own journey to greatness right now. Some sweet, beautiful children somewhere are waiting on you.

Be great. Plan like a PIRATE.

Find exclusive chapter resources and more
Plan Like a PIRATE information here:

educationundone.com

Works Referenced

Baldwin, James. *Collected Essays*. New York: Library of America, 1998.

Blumberg, Naomi. "Malala Yousafzai." In *Encyclopedia Britannica*. Accessed April 29, 2021. britannica.com/biography/Malala-Yousafzai.

Burgess, Dave. *Teach Like a PIRATE: Increase Student Engagement, Boost Your Creativity, and Transform Your Life as an Educator*. San Diegeo, CA: Dave Burgess Consulting, 2018.

Casas, Jimmy. *Culturize: Every Student, Every Day, Whatever It Takes*. San Diego, CA: Dave Burgess Consulting, 2017.

Francis, Erik M. "Depth of Knowledge or Extent of Learning." Maverik Education blog. 2018. https://maverikeducation.com/blog/f/depth-of-knowledge-or-extent-of-learning.

Fulghum, Robert. *All I Really Need to Know I Learned in Kindergarten: Uncommon Thoughts on Common Things*. New York: Ballantine Books, 2004.

Gardner, Howard. *Frames of Mind: The Theory of Multiple Intelligences*. New York: Basic Books, 2011.

Hess, Karin. "Cognitive Rigor and DOK Focus Area." Educational Research in Action. Last modified July 2014. karin-hess.com/cognitive-rigor-and-dok.

Houf, Beth, and Shelley Burgess. *Lead Like a PIRATE: Make School Amazing for Your Students and Staff*. San Diego, CA: Dave Burgess Consulting, 2017.

Lassiter, Cathy J. *Everyday Courage for School Leaders*. Thousand Oaks, CA: Corwin, 2017.

Lewis-Clark State College. "Teaching Antiracism." Center for Teaching and Learning. lcsc.edu/teaching-learning/inclusion-diversity -equity-antiracism/teaching-antiracism.

Manhattan Prep. *5 Lb. Book of ACT Practice Problems*. New York: Manhattan Prep Publishing, 2015.

Martin, Tara. *Be REAL: Educate from the Heart*. San Diego, CA: Dave Burgess Consulting, 2018.

Meehan, Robert J. *Teacher's Journey: The Road Less Traveled*. Mustang, OK: Tate Pub & Enterprises, 2011.

Moss, Connie M., and Susan M. Brookhart. *Learning Targets: Helping Students Aim for Understanding in Today's Lesson*. Alexandria, VA: Association for Supervision and Curriculum Development, 2012.

National Governors Association Center for Best Practices, Council of Chief State School. *Common Core State Standards*. English Language Arts Standards/History/Social Studies/Grade 6–8. National Governors Association Center for Best Practices, Council of Chief State School Officers, Washington, DC, 2010.

Ohio Association for Gifted Children. *What to Expect When . . . You're Teaching a Gifted Child: A Handbook for Teachers of Gifted Children*. OAGC. 2013. oagc.com/wp-content/uploads/2021/07/ WHAT-TO-EXPECT...Teacher-Handbook-8.24.2018.pdf.

Pierson, Rita. "Every Kid Needs a Champion." TED Talks Education. May 2013. www.ted.com/talks/rita_pierson_every_kid_needs_a _champion/transcript?language=en.

Portnoy, Lindsay. *Designed to Learn*: *Using Design Thinking to Bring Purpose and Passion to Learn to the Classroom*. Alexandria, VA: Association for Supervision and Curriculum Development, 2020.

Sims Bishop, R. "Mirrors, Windows, and Sliding Glass Doors." *Perspectives* 1, no. 3 (1990): ix–xi.

Strunk, William, Jr., and E. B. White. *The Elements of Style*. New York: Pearson, 2019.

Study Finds. "Third of Adults Still Sleep with 'Comfort Object' from Childhood, Survey Shows." Study Finds. June 12, 2019. studyfinds. org/third-adults-sleep-comfort-object-childhood/.

Tomlinson, Carol A. *The Differentiated Classroom: Responding to the Needs of All Learners*. Alexandria, VA: Association for Supervision and Curriculum Development, 1999.

United Nations Educational, Scientific, and Cultural Organization (UNESCO). *Declaration of Principles on Tolerance*. UNESCO General Session 28, Paris, November 16, 1995.

Wiggins, Grant P., and Jay McTighe. *Understanding by Design*. Alexandria, VA: Association for Supervision and Curriculum Development, 2008.

ACKNOWLEDGMENTS

"For we are God's handiwork, created in Christ Jesus to do good works, which God prepared in advance for us to do."

—EPHESIANS 2:10, NIV

First and foremost, I want to give thanks to God for the blessings, knowledge, and opportunities He endlessly provides. Without His love, grace, and limitless promises, nothing would be possible. Fulfilling this dream has always been part of His plan.

To John and Johnny, my husband and our son, your love is what keeps me going every single day. Without your support and encouragement, your patience and understanding, I would never have been able to accomplish this. This book is yours as much as it is mine. Thank you both for loving me and for always being there for me. I love you.

I am grateful to Dave and Shelley Burgess for their belief in my message and for helping make one of my biggest dreams become a reality. Getting to know you both has been life changing and has brought me such joy. I am eternally thankful to Tara Martin for being the most uplifting and knowledgeable coach of all time and to Liz Schreiter for her magnificent creativity in helping to bring the vision of my message to life in so many ways. I'm deeply thankful to the entire DBC family for all of their support.

To Sal and the editing team, I am eternally indebted for your commitment to keeping my manifesto true to my own voice and for keeping me moving in the right direction throughout the entire editing process. Your careful attentiveness to my words let me know that my work was in the right hands. For that I am deeply grateful.

To my dear friend, Traci Browder, I can't tell you enough how I appreciate your encouragement, and especially your beautiful prayers, which keep me going to this day. I'm so happy that you have been part of this journey with me.

Last, and certainly not least, I am thankful for every student that has ever set foot in my classroom. This book exists because your lives and your stories captured my heart in ways that pushed me to be the best for each of you. I am blessed to have been your teacher.

Bring Dawn to Your School!

Dawn's professional teaching experiences have been showcased in scholarly journals and at local, regional, national, and international conferences. Prior to becoming an educator, Dawn spent more than ten years in marketing and publishing in the private sector. This experience has given Dawn insight into the skills and knowledge students need in order to be prepared to enter into a competitive, global workforce or into college once they leave high school. These insights help Dawn in supporting veteran, novice, and pre-service teachers as they seek to educate students for tomorrow's work today. As a licensed curriculum, instruction, and professional development specialist, Dawn's primary goal in all things is to support educators with planning learning that ignites curiosity and that engages and inspires students in a way that impacts their growth and achievement every single day.

ANTIRACISM EDUCATION

- Backward Designing Antiracism Education (K-12)
- Intentionally Designed Villages: Creating Diverse Teaching Teams to Promote Inclusion (K-12)
- Exploring Diversity through Dystopian Literature (7-12 ELA)

LESSON PLANNING AND CURRICULUM DESIGN

- Essential Planning Practices to Engage, Inspire, and Grow Students Every Day (7-12)
- Planning High, Deep, and Wide: Differentiating in the Gifted Classroom (K-12)
- Not Just Tech for Tech's Sake: Purposeful Use of Technology to Engage and Assess (K-12)

PROJECT-BASED, INCLUSIVE LEARNING DESIGN

- The Credo Project: Comprehensive Language and Literacy Study (7-12 ELA)
- Problem-Based Service Learning with Passion Projects (7-12)
- Improving Language and Literacy with Performance-Based Assessments (7-12)

EDUCATOR PROFESSIONAL GROWTH

- Goal Planning for Infinite Impact In and Out of the Classroom
- Your Best Evaluation Yet

Please contact Dawn via email to learn more about consulting and speaking opportunities:

dawn@educationundone.com

ABOUT DAWN

Dawn Harris is a passionate and energetic educator who lives by the motto, "Relationships First." Her enthusiasm for creating connections is infectious and she thrives on the opportunity to learn about the things that motivate and inspire teachers and students alike. In her roles as a secondary English language arts educator, gifted and talented teacher, and associate professor of teacher education, Dawn continually strives to bring authentic and engaging learning experiences to students of all ages.

Throughout her career as an educator, Dawn has taught in urban, rural, and suburban districts meeting the needs of children from a wide range of backgrounds and cultures. In addition to general ELA coursework, Dawn's classroom teaching experience also includes teaching English as a second language, creative writing, film studies, and response to intervention instruction.

MORE FROM

DAVE BURGESS Consulting, Inc.

Since 2012, DBCI has published books that inspire and equip educators to be their best. For more information on our titles or to purchase bulk orders for your school, district, or book study, visit **DaveBurgessConsulting.com/DBCIbooks**.

Like a PIRATE™ Series

Teach Like a PIRATE by Dave Burgess
eXPlore Like a PIRATE by Michael Matera
Learn Like a PIRATE by Paul Solarz
Play Like a PIRATE by Quinn Rollins
Run Like a PIRATE by Adam Welcome
Tech Like a PIRATE by Matt Miller

Lead Like a PIRATE™ Series

Lead Like a PIRATE by Shelley Burgess and Beth Houf
Balance Like a PIRATE by Jessica Cabeen, Jessica Johnson, and
    Sarah Johnson
Lead beyond Your Title by Nili Bartley
Lead with Appreciation by Amber Teamann and Melinda Miller
Lead with Culture by Jay Billy
Lead with Instructional Rounds by Vicki Wilson
Lead with Literacy by Mandy Ellis

Leadership & School Culture

Beyond the Surface of Restorative Practices by Marisol Rerucha
Choosing to See by Pamela Seda and Kyndall Brown
Culturize by Jimmy Casas

Discipline Win by Andy Jacks

Escaping the School Leader's Dunk Tank by Rebecca Coda and
    Rick Jetter

Fight Song by Kim Bearden

From Teacher to Leader by Starr Sackstein

If the Dance Floor Is Empty, Change the Song by Joe Clark

The Innovator's Mindset by George Couros

It's OK to Say "They" by Christy Whittlesey

Kids Deserve It! by Todd Nesloney and Adam Welcome

Let Them Speak by Rebecca Coda and Rick Jetter

The Limitless School by Abe Hege and Adam Dovico

Live Your Excellence by Jimmy Casas

Next-Level Teaching by Jonathan Alsheimer

The Pepper Effect by Sean Gaillard

Principaled by Kate Barker, Kourtney Ferrua, and Rachael George

The Principled Principal by Jeffrey Zoul and Anthony McConnell

Relentless by Hamish Brewer

The Secret Solution by Todd Whitaker, Sam Miller, and Ryan Donlan

Start. Right. Now. by Todd Whitaker, Jeffrey Zoul, and Jimmy Casas

Stop. Right. Now. by Jimmy Casas and Jeffrey Zoul

Teachers Deserve It by Rae Hughart and Adam Welcome

Teach Your Class Off by CJ Reynolds

They Call Me "Mr. De" by Frank DeAngelis

Thrive Through the Five by Jill M. Siler

Unmapped Potential by Julie Hasson and Missy Lennard

When Kids Lead by Todd Nesloney and Adam Dovico

Word Shift by Joy Kirr

Your School Rocks by Ryan McLane and Eric Lowe

Technology & Tools

50 Things to Go Further with Google Classroom by Alice Keeler and
    Libbi Miller

50 Things You Can Do with Google Classroom by Alice Keeler and
    Libbi Miller

140 Twitter Tips for Educators by Brad Currie, Billy Krakower, and
    Scott Rocco

Block Breaker by Brian Aspinall

Building Blocks for Tiny Techies by Jamila "Mia" Leonard

Code Breaker by Brian Aspinall

The Complete EdTech Coach by Katherine Goyette and Adam Juarez

Control Alt Achieve by Eric Curts

The Esports Education Playbook by Chris Aviles, Steve Isaacs, Christine
    Lion-Bailey, and Jesse Lubinsky

Google Apps for Littles by Christine Pinto and Alice Keeler

Master the Media by Julie Smith

Raising Digital Leaders by Jennifer Casa-Todd

Reality Bytes by Christine Lion-Bailey, Jesse Lubinsky, and
    Micah Shippee, PhD

Sail the 7 Cs with Microsoft Education by Becky Keene and
    Kathi Kersznowski

Shake Up Learning by Kasey Bell

Social LEADia by Jennifer Casa-Todd

Stepping Up to Google Classroom by Alice Keeler and
    Kimberly Mattina

Teaching Math with Google Apps by Alice Keeler and Diana Herrington

Teachingland by Amanda Fox and Mary Ellen Weeks

Teaching with Google Jamboard by Alice Keeler and Kimberly Mattina

Teaching Methods & Materials

All 4s and 5s by Andrew Sharos

Boredom Busters by Katie Powell

The Classroom Chef by John Stevens and Matt Vaudrey

The Collaborative Classroom by Trevor Muir

Copyrighteous by Diana Gill

CREATE by Bethany J. Petty

Ditch That Homework by Matt Miller and Alice Keeler

Ditch That Textbook by Matt Miller

Don't Ditch That Tech by Matt Miller, Nate Ridgway, and Angelia Ridgway

EDrenaline Rush by John Meehan

Educated by Design by Michael Cohen, The Tech Rabbi

The EduProtocol Field Guide by Marlena Hebern and Jon Corippo

The EduProtocol Field Guide: Book 2 by Marlena Hebern and Jon Corippo

The EduProtocol Field Guide: Math Edition by Lisa Nowakowski and Jeremiah Ruesch

Expedition Science by Becky Schnekser

Frustration Busters by Katie Powell

Fully Engaged by Michael Matera and John Meehan

Game On? Brain On! by Lindsay Portnoy, PhD

Guided Math AMPED by Reagan Tunstall

Innovating Play by Jessica LaBar-Twomy and Christine Pinto

Instant Relevance by Denis Sheeran

Keeping the Wonder by Jenna Copper, Ashley Bible, Abby Gross, and Staci Lamb

LAUNCH by John Spencer and A.J. Juliani

Make Learning MAGICAL by Tisha Richmond

Pass the Baton by Kathryn Finch and Theresa Hoover

Project-Based Learning Anywhere by Lori Elliott

Pure Genius by Don Wettrick

The Revolution by Darren Ellwein and Derek McCoy

Shift This! by Joy Kirr

Skyrocket Your Teacher Coaching by Michael Cary Sonbert

Spark Learning by Ramsey Musallam

Sparks in the Dark by Travis Crowder and Todd Nesloney

Table Talk Math by John Stevens

Unpack Your Impact by Naomi O'Brien and LaNesha Tabb

The Wild Card by Hope and Wade King

The Writing on the Classroom Wall by Steve Wyborney

You Are Poetry by Mike Johnston

Inspiration, Professional Growth & Personal Development

Be REAL by Tara Martin

Be the One for Kids by Ryan Sheehy

The Coach ADVenture by Amy Illingworth

Creatively Productive by Lisa Johnson

Educational Eye Exam by Alicia Ray

The EduNinja Mindset by Jennifer Burdis

Empower Our Girls by Lynmara Colón and Adam Welcome

Finding Lifelines by Andrew Grieve and Andrew Sharos

The Four O'Clock Faculty by Rich Czyz

How Much Water Do We Have? by Pete and Kris Nunweiler

P Is for Pirate by Dave and Shelley Burgess

A Passion for Kindness by Tamara Letter

The Path to Serendipity by Allyson Apsey

Sanctuaries by Dan Tricarico

Saving Sycamore by Molly B. Hudgens

The SECRET SAUCE by Rich Czyz

Shattering the Perfect Teacher Myth by Aaron Hogan

Stories from Webb by Todd Nesloney

Talk to Me by Kim Bearden

Teach Better by Chad Ostrowski, Tiffany Ott, Rae Hughart, and Jeff Gargas

Teach Me, Teacher by Jacob Chastain

Teach, Play, Learn! by Adam Peterson

The Teachers of Oz by Herbie Raad and Nathan Lang-Raad

TeamMakers by Laura Robb and Evan Robb

Through the Lens of Serendipity by Allyson Apsey

The Zen Teacher by Dan Tricarico

Children's Books

Beyond Us by Aaron Polansky

Cannonball In by Tara Martin

Dolphins in Trees by Aaron Polansky

I Can Achieve Anything by MoNique Waters

I Want to Be a Lot by Ashley Savage

The Princes of Serendip by Allyson Apsey

Ride with Emilio by Richard Nares

The Wild Card Kids by Hope and Wade King

Zom-Be a Design Thinker by Amanda Fox

CPSIA information can be obtained
at www.ICGtesting.com
Printed in the USA
JSHW011129080722
27793JS00006B/173